BUILDING
BERLIN

THE LATEST ARCHITECTURE IN AND OUT OF THE CAPITAL

Highly productive, no compromises

Pauses in running operations are a good time for creative contemplation. Designing architects are good at using even slack periods productively and thinking ahead. Throughout the history of building, periods of economic decline are regarded as especially valuable – as incubators of renewal in the building culture. When the construction industry was on its knees in 1918, the Glass Chain architects led by the Taut and Luckhardt brothers, Gropius and Scharoun discussed the contribution that architecture could make to the new age. Gropius pointedly described the situation as being a mixture of "reaching for the stars and everyday work". By the time the building boom began during the Weimar Republic, the cornerstones of Modern architecture had already been established.

Similarly, the successful Berlin joint building ventures with which many colleagues created their own commissions during the lean years after the turn of the millennium can also be regarded as a laboratory of ideas. Ideally, these could benefit housing construction and urban development to this day. However, it takes significant efforts by everyone involved to maintain high quality standards under the considerable production pressure prevailing today.

Whether quality cycles of this kind exist is a matter of debate. However, it is certain that the building industry is currently booming and the order books of many offices are full. Moreover, we certainly do not yearn for a return to those days of enforced contemplation, since they are above all times of shortages and a lack of income. But how can such times, when the market is crying out for our services, actually move us forward? Fortunately, architects are no longer automatically expected to deliver grand ideas for small fees. Whoever wants innovation in the future will have to invest accordingly to provide the necessary room for manoeuvre. Perhaps even the honorarium code HOAI could once again serve the purpose of capping fees, as was its original intention.

So it is all the more surprising that despite their good business situation, many architects are gladly willing to participate in planning competitions, be it out of sporting ambition or as a way of working on the most exciting projects. Sensible clients will appreciate this way of contracting good architects, thereby also giving smaller offices a chance. Firstly, they are more likely to have free capacities. Secondly, such offices are committed and always willing to put their hearts and souls into the project. They may even have an advantage in the search for qualified personnel: employees like working where they assume full responsibility and are not merely a cog in the machine. After all, Bruno Taut's goal of the past remains equally relevant today: "Let us consciously be imaginary architects!"

Christine Edmaier
President of the Berlin Chamber of Architects

Residential

Office, Commerce & Trade

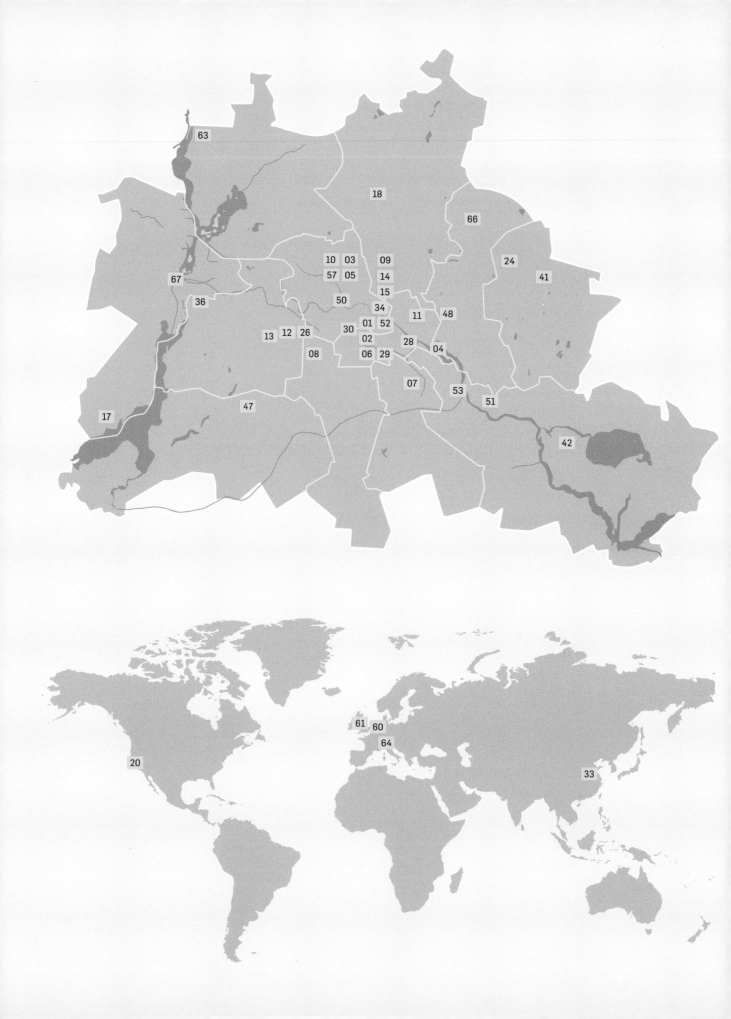

Projects in and from Berlin

This book presents 67 projects by members of Berlin's Chamber of Architects completed in Berlin and further afield prior to summer 2018. The collection encompasses works of architecture, interior design, landscape architecture and urban planning. This selection was curated by a panel of seven experts: the Hamburg urban planner Jörn Walter, Jutta Wakob, landscape architect in Cologne, Oliver Platz, President of the Bremen Chamber of Architects, the Berlin journalist Brigitte Fehrle, the interior designer Dorothée Meier and the architect Peter Haimerl, both from Munich, and Christine Edmaier as President of the Berlin Chamber of Architects.

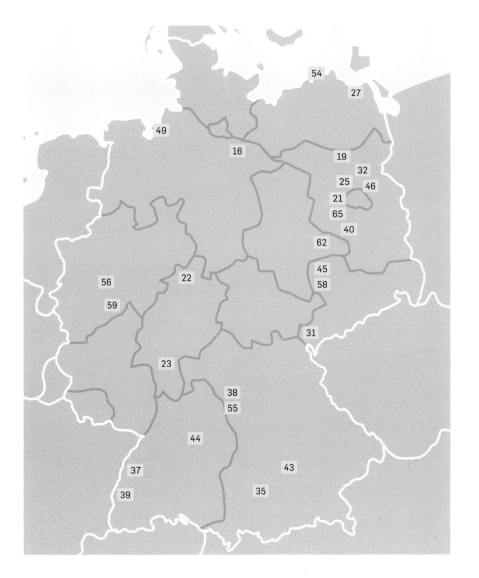

01	to	23	Residential
24	to	35	Office, Commerce & Trade
36	to	39	Infrastructure & Mobility
40	to	42	Health, Leisure & Social Services
43	to	49	Education & Science
50	to	54	Culture
55	to	65	Open Space
66	to	67	Urban Planning

Listed building projects
04 21 22 28 29 31 32 36
45 48 62 67

Sustainable building projects
14 16 18 24 32 42 45 50
54 66

Interior design
05 15 26 27 28 29 31 35

Densification
01 02 03 05 06 07 08 09
10 11 12 13 14 17 18 30
31 34 44 45 46 47 51 52
54 66

Completed competition projects
16 23 30 31 37 38 47 49
50 55 56 57 58 59

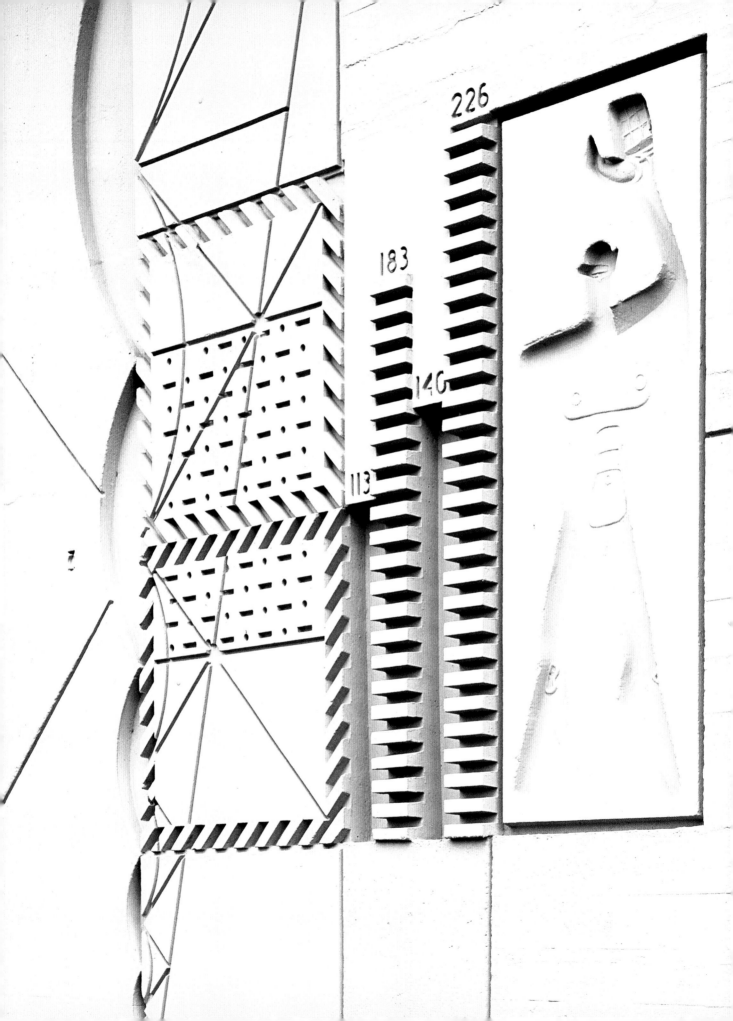

100 years of modular building
Developing quality housing despite limited time and funds

Modulor proportion system by Le Corbusier at the Corbusierhaus Berlin (left), crate bar at the Kraftwerk Berlin

Berlin requires no less than 30,000 new homes every year. The annual volume of planned housing units in Germany is 350,000. For years, policymakers have neglected housing construction, but suddenly, everything must happen at great speed and low cost. Yet the economy and the industry are not prepared for such growth.

Hardly a day passes without a debate on the housing issue somewhere in the country, with participating planners, politicians and builders proposing ways out of the crisis. Modules and standard types are often discussed in this context, with references to buildings from the 1920s and 1930s, as well as the Bauhaus period, when designing architects experimented with industrialised building techniques all around the world. Some discourse even focuses on major post-war housing estates. "One design, multiple building" appears to be the miracle-mantra of the times. But does standardisation really guarantee cost-efficiency and speed? And what does it mean for housing quality?

Standard, type, module and series – everyone interprets all these terms differently. The real estate industry juggles them as it pleases to suit its marketing jargon and even architects have begun to appropriate them in this way. It is almost as if anything at the building site that is not delivered in sacks is described as a module...

Let us try to clarify the situation. Standardisation can refer to a wide range of building aspects: the planning process, the building process or the housing product, as Andrea Benze, Julia Gill and Saskia Hebert explain in their study of serial housing development that was commissioned by the Berlin Senate ahead of the planned IBA 2020. As well as defining terms, the study investigates the extent to which industrial prefabrication and modern technologies make the series flexible. With respect to housing construction, standardisation means using normed building elements and materials. However, when the term is used in planning, it mostly refers to typical floor plans and standard details. For instance a module can be a bath delivered to a building site, a complete apartment or a wall including pre-fitted windows.

John Klepel from the Berlin office LIN Architekten Urbanisten, which has developed standard high-rise housing for the HOWOGE housing association, states: "The term 'type' does not yet have the same connotations as the term 'series' for instance, which implies repetition. Type refers to a framework that is flexible and can incorporate many different programmes. There is a touch of type in our standard high-rise housing, but it also includes prefabrication and modular building." Christoph Roedig and his office roedig.schop architekten have planned apartment buildings for the state-owned housing association Stadt und Land Wohnbauten-Gesellschaft. He believes typification does

Deutscher Bauherrenpreis 2018: "Ausbauhaus" in Neukölln by Praeger Richter Architekten

not mean making everything look the same: "Today, mass customisation makes it possible to adapt details without extra investment. It is irrelevant to carpentries whether windows are all the same size. Their machines are computer-controlled." His partner Ulrich Schop comments: "A standard building is not a contemporary answer to today's complex society. After all,

standard travel offers have also disappeared from the market. Nowadays you click on 17 different options. There's no such thing as a simple package to Mallorca and back."

Due to their experiences of monotony in major housing estates, some people fear that the current trend towards standardisation will lead to a lack of quality. But there are many answers to the question of what quality in housing development means today. They start with the residents. While some discuss open floor plans, communal spaces and commercial uses on the ground floor, others focus more on what the authorities pay for and what not. "When building rented apartments for housing associations, we are dealing with a different clientele compared to privately funded housing or joint building ventures", Ulrich Schop explains. Housing associations are large bodies with many departments. The spatial programme is not defined by the planners, but by the customer centres that digitally analyse resident enquiries. As Schop explains, when planning for housing associations, architects feel as if they spend 90 percent of their time fulfilling predefined criteria. Working on the floor plan is a matter of square centimetres that have an effect on public funding, but that leads to questions such as: "Does every bedroom really need a three-metre cupboard space and must every bed be two metres wide?" Then there are customer preferences that naturally tend towards already established tastes. Aspects such as fairfaced concrete, corridors without skirting boards and flooring without laminate in a wood look are all equally difficult to imagine. Schop would welcome greater flexibility from housing associations in defining their expectations: "We should work to increase awareness in this respect and be more audacious. Some people must be challenged to try out new things. That is also an aspect of quality."

For the housing market, quality seems more to be a question of costs per square metre. In the summer of 2017, the GdW, an umbrella housing organisation, jointly announced a competition with the Federal Ministry of Building, the Federal Chamber of Architects and the building industry to develop innovative serial construction concepts. 50 bidding consortiums consisting of architectural offices and building companies applied, of which nine won awards. Results were disappointing in the category "Innovation". Four of the nine entries proposed a thermal insulation system, while most used classic reinforced concrete elements. The GdW regards the results as a success: "The proposed prices for the nine model buildings are between 2,000 and 3,000 Euros per square metre of floor space, which is lower than the average production costs for apartment buildings in Germany", the organisation's website states. The Federal Chamber of Architects was less enthusiastic about the results. "The building types presented here can only be part of the solution in creating as many affordable apartments as possible. To close

Serial individuality: Social housing in Kreuzberg's Lindenstrasse

existing gaps in desirable cities and prevent greater land con-sumption, we will require different intelligent tools to further strengthen housing development and also help accelerate the small-scale insertion of new apartments in urban areas", the Chamber's President, Barbara Ettinger-Brinckmann, commented.

Finn Geipel from the office LIN Architekten Urbanisten believes that quality in housing construction is initially a matter of urban planning. One must ask the questions: Where will we build apartments: in greenfields or in existing neighbourhoods? How well is the housing connected to public transport? How good are local supplies and services, and what qualities exist in the surrounding open spaces? Once densification plans become known in the neighbourhood, residents usually try to resist them. New green and playing areas, bicycle parking spaces and shopping facilities that arrive in the quarter with the new housing

can increase its acceptance. There will be a change of gener-ations in many 1960s and 1970s estates. LIN Architekten Urba-nisten have provided ideas to the Bremen housing association Gewoba on how people can grow old in their apartments and still allow young people to move into the estate: bridges can connect new point buildings to existing structures that have no lifts, allowing old people to remain in their apartments despite needing a walker or wheelchair. In the meantime, the sixth point building is being erected in Bremen, but unfortunately none of them have a bridge.

"The access situation and the relationship to the surroundings also determine the quality of housing", Finn Geipel explains. Staircases and elevator cores define the flexibility of apartment sizes. Geipel often plans apartments with two entrances. He believes that the speed with which new housing is built is a further aspect of quality. A timber structure with a shell that is built in one month is less of a burden on the neighbourhood than constructing with in-situ cast concrete.

Can standard buildings save time and money? In 2017, the six state-owned housing associations in Berlin commissioned studies for high-rise buildings, point buildings, roof structures, blocks and rows. A thick brochure summarises the results, but little has actually been built so far. Only the Stadt und Land Wohn-bauten-Gesellschaft, which has been constructing 165 rental apartments in the district of Marzahn-Hellersdorf since April 2018, speaks of standard building using housing modules. The recipe is to design only a few reinforced concrete walls and many more supports to allow variable floor plans, prefabricated bathrooms and staircases, and brick-insulated exterior walls. Variety is achieved using various plasters, colours, windows and balconies.

The Berlin architect Marc Frohn from FAR believes that quality in housing construction can be measured by the extent to which the floor plans can cope with the diversity of living models. In Berlin, he is currently erecting an apartment building with pre-fabricated concrete elements that are usually produced for industrial factories. The advantage is that the large spans ensure maximum freedom for the floor plans. With respect to saving costs, Frohn explained that everything is extremely relative and there are no general answers. He stated that the high level of prefabrication had a positive effect on costs, but only when the design follows the rules of prefabrication and no individual alterations are planned. Frohn spent much time appropriating the logic of building elements and production in a factory before applying it to his apartment building. The six floors of his shell construction can be erected in only six and a half weeks.

Having flexible floor plans does not just mean being able to divide large apartments into several smaller ones and vice versa. Flexibility can also be expressed within an apartment – for instance when room plans are designed in a way that allows them to assume different functions: when bedrooms can become children's rooms as the family develops, when a study can also be used as a second child's room, or when a room can be partitioned to provide more privacy to children of different ages, and generally when a mother, father and two children are only one of many models, rather than the standard.

In view of the many handbooks on building types and projects published on the Internet, one could almost get the impression that architects will soon be superfluous to housing development, especially since the rise of demands for an open-source floor-plan database. But will housing associations soon merely place finished designs onto individual properties? "There is noth-

1960s Systembox K67 by the Slovenian architect Saša J. Mächtig

ing better than rebuilding a good floor plan. But that is always only a snapshot", Christoph Roedig explains. "Since Modernity, architects have always thought they've got it now. And then energy-savings regulations change and you start all over again. There is no such thing as a general solution."

One design, multiple building – today's situation is not as simple as the 60s and 70s credo. Major housing estates are not a role model for fast, cheap building. Firstly, society has changed: families are not all the same, an apartment is no longer for life, and surroundings and transport networks have become more important. Secondly, we can no longer build in the same volumes because such large open areas in the city no longer exist. Thirdly, building on the free market is different from social housing development or the socialist planned economy. For instance modules are only economic until the market has recognised that every-

Prototypes for GDR standard buildings in Berlin, early 1990s

one wants them and consequently raises their price. "It's like oil and gas", Christoph Roedig explains. So clients should consider exactly where a module is suitable, what size is appropriate and who should produce it.

However, there are ways out of the cul de sac we find ourselves in due to the pressures of costs and time. We constantly invent new norms and standards, think we can retain that much-vaunted flexibility through standard buildings and believe that colours, balcony types and front door varieties can fulfil the demand for diversity. As naïve as it sounds, we have to respond to society's diversity with our own diversity and communication. More architectural competitions would be one option. Spreading awareness among residents is another. Involving tenants at an early stage (as a number of housing associations are already doing) is a third. Perhaps we should stop thinking in types, series and

standards altogether since it places the technocratic aspect of Modernity on a pedestal as a paradigm. Perhaps instead, we should apply terms such as diversity and flexibility to our structures. What if we started to seek flexibility in the requirements and mindsets of the major housing associations? What if we experimented more and regarded the diversity of residents as a form of potential? And what if we not only brought those involved and their fields together at the drawing board, but also let them live and work together, as the Bauhaus movement once did? It made Bauhaus world-famous.

Metropolenhaus am Jüdischen Museum

Markgrafenstrasse 88
10969 Berlin

GFA 8,650 m²
GV 27,675 m³

bfstudio-architekten GbR
bfstudio-architekten.de

Client: METROPOLENHAUS
Am Jüdischen Museum GmbH & Co. KG

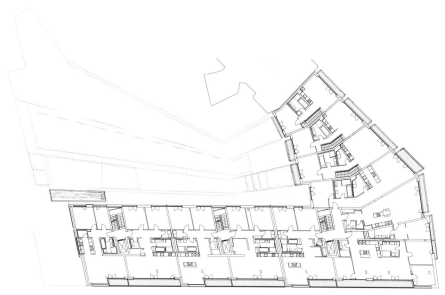

Second floor plan

View from the square

New development with apartments, studios, stores, gastronomic services and a cultural platform. The successful use concept was developed in a concept process to determine the property's allocation. The underlying idea is to revitalise the neighbourhood with an active ground floor including shops, gastronomic services and project rooms in an open cultural platform with rents capped at six Euros per square metre. The ground floor was cross-financed by the sale of other units. On the first floor, ten units are prioritised for creative-sector use, while the upper floors accommodate 37 apartments and maisonettes, as well as four units for living and working. The new building's architecture is based on the historical urban structure: towards Markgrafenstrasse, its structure recalls the former parcelling. All units have barrier-free access via three staircases and broad pergolas.

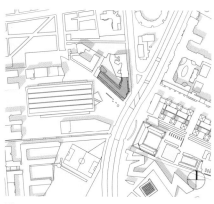

Plan

Apartment (top), view from the garden (bottom)

IBeB – Integrative building project at the former wholesale flower market

Lindenstrasse 90/91
10969 Berlin

GFA 12,275 m²
GV 42,125 m³

ARGE ifau | HEIDE & VON BECKERATH
www.ifau.berlin.heimat.de
www.heidevonbeckerath.com

Client: IBeB GbR (Selbstbaugenossenschaft Berlin eG | Ev. Gemeindeverein der Gehörlosen in Berlin e. V. | private owners)

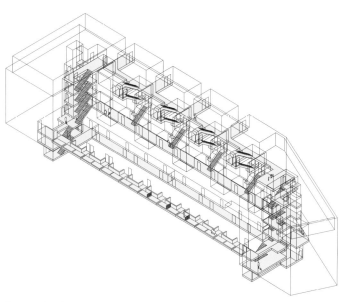

Access structure

Apartment

Rue intérieure on the first floor

New development with apartments, studios and commercial spaces. The project uses concept-based property allocation in the new neighbourhood at the former wholesale flower market in Berlin Kreuzberg. Binding development standards, as well as the type and situation of common areas were coordinated with all participants at the outset: private owners, a cooperative and a social institution. Three horizontal accessing routes connected through staircases and five atria form the underlying structure of the building logic. That inner structure determined the system and proportions of the units, which were planned together with their users. The cooperative apartments and studios were cross-financed to ensure fixed rent prices. The result was a total of 66 individual apartments in a wide range of types, as well as 17 studios, which were presented to users as "blanks", and three commercial units.

View from the northeast (top), studio (bottom)

H6 – New prefab

Hochstrasse 7
13357 Berlin

GFA 5,000 m²
GV 16,525 m³

**ARGE H6 (roedig.schop architekten,
sieglundalbert architekten)**
www.roedig-schop.de
www.sieglundalbert.de

Client: Joint planning and building venture
Hochstrasse 6

View from the Volkspark Humboldthain

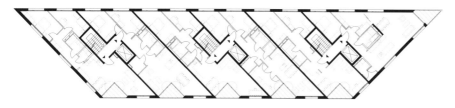

Fifth floor plan

New construction of an apartment building for a joint building venture. From an aerial perspective, the trapeze-shaped structure is situated within the junction branches of two railway lines. Despite good connections and increasing demand for building land, no-one had shown particular interest in the triangular property when it was placed on the market in 2014, apart from the joint venture. A sandwich façade made of prefabricated concrete elements gives the building sufficient mass to cope with the noise and vibrations. The floor plans follow an axis grid of 3.16 metres that is binding for all parties. The resulting 36 apartments aligned in a north-south direction have sizes between 60 and 115 square metres. Three staircases each provide access to two apartments on all of the six floors. Towards the north (facing the S-Bahn circle line), the house is positioned like a protective wall. Loggias facing the southern garden reveal a view of the Volkspark Humboldthain that cannot be obstructed by future development.

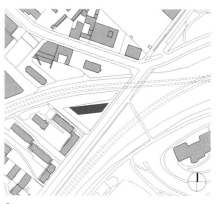

Plan

Apartment with loggia (top), view from the S-Bahn circle line and street (bottom)

Alt-Stralau glassworks

Glasbläserallee 13–17
10245 Berlin

GFA (after conversion)   980 m²
GFA (before conversion) 3,350 m²
GV (after conversion)   1,875 m³
GV (before conversion) 14,075 m³

Eyrich-Hertweck Architekten
www.eharchitekten.de

Client: Baugruppe Glashütte Alt-Stralau

Kitchen

Apartment entrance area

Renovated staircase

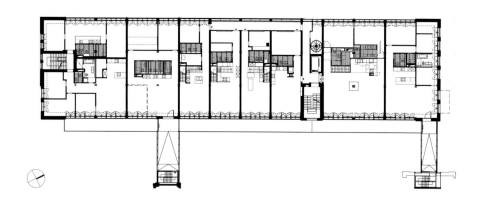

First floor plan

Conversion of a listed building as a joint building venture. For over 100 years, glass was manufactured and processed on the Stralau peninsula. Production ended in the mid-1990s. The conversion of the factory building erected in 1923 created 25 apartments and one commercial unit. The walled-up windows were opened and the building's exterior was restored to resemble its original appearance. The building's characteristic steel structure has also remained visible. A new shell made of ecological materials was added behind the historical façade. Dark zinc façades with large windows envelop the formerly open ground floor, as well as the new attic level, recalling the previous bitumen roof. By contrast, new additions such as the balconies are clad in rusty steel.

View from the north (top), ground floor residential workshop (bottom)

Housing in Chausseestrasse

Chausseestrasse 48a
10115 Berlin

GFA 1,100 m²
GV 3,550 m³

**Wietersheim Architekten
Partnerschaftsgesellschaft mbB**
www.wietersheim.com

Client: private

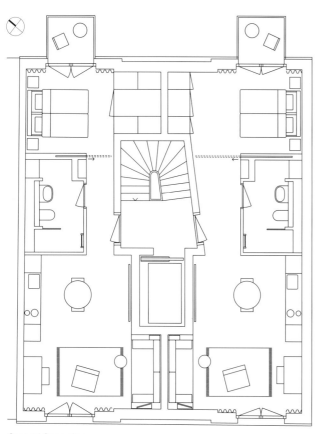

Second floor plan

Alcoves

New development of an inner-urban apartment building. The head-end structure of a block perimeter adjoins with an open development from the post-war period. The headquarters of the Federal Intelligence Service dominate opposite – a vis-à-vis with 14,000 windows. The new building's exterior appearance reveals its load-bearing structure: the ceilings support rectangular wall blocks resembling slabs. The monolithic elements consist of core-insulated bricks. Room-high windows highlight the distances between the wall elements. The ground floor accommodates a shop and provides a broad entrance to the buildings behind. 11 apartments cover the six upper levels. Their staircase core organises the floor plans into kitchen, living and bedroom areas. Partitions, sliding doors, wardrobes and alcoves were installed as wooden fittings.

View from the street (top), sliding door, living room, view from the courtyard (bottom)

Heightened building in Berlin-Kreuzberg

Wassertorstrasse 12–13
10969 Berlin

GFA 445 m²
GV 2,225 m³

buchner + wienke and
Architekturbüro Martina Trixner
www.buchnerundwienke.de
www.martina-trixner.de

Client: Wassertorstrasse GbR

Rooftop terrace

View from the street

Fifth floor section and plan

Joint building venture on a post-war modern apartment building. The housing block is situated outside the desirable old town neighbourhoods in a 1970s redevelopment area. The clients agreed that the urban planning situation, the urban asperity of the location and the broad courtyard with lush vegetation had their own qualities in themselves. Thus they decided to condense the development without occupying additional ground. The new rooftop extension accommodates five apartments with varying sizes, four of which have a gallery level and a rooftop terrace. The load-bearing structure and the exterior envelope are timber constructions with wooden supports, wallboard layers and solid wood elements. The supports, beams and ceilings in the apartments remain without cladding and have merely been leached and oil-varnished in white.

Floating Penthouse

Hertzbergstrasse 31
12055 Berlin

GFA 165 m²
GV 500 m³

Atelier Zafari
www.atelier-zafari.com

Client: private

Building rear view

Terrace towards the street

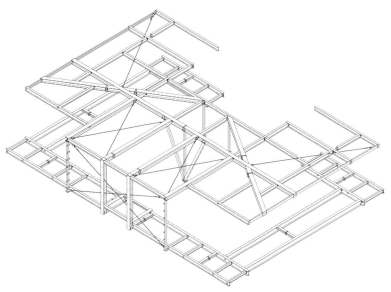

Load-bearing structure

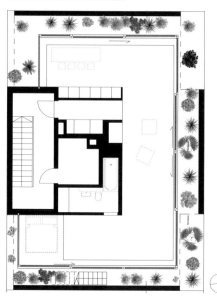

Floor plan

Rooftop development for a 1970s apartment building. The 80 square metre penthouse sets itself apart from the existing structure as a black vertical extension. Since the original structure was not strong enough to support the new level, it was constructed as a broadly spanned, floating framework. The complex steel skeleton clad in trapezoidal sheet metal is anchored to the walls of the neighbouring buildings to reduce the load on the rooftop. A glazed terrace with a further 40 square metres is integrated into the structure. Like the living area, it is spread around three sides of a core consisting of a bathroom, wardrobe/entrance area, technical equipment and the stairs. From a legal perspective, the development was planned as a staggered floor covering two thirds of the area. In some interior areas, the differentiated floor plan and platforms reduce the room height to such an extent that it is not considered as living space. This maximises the defined capacity and optimises the interaction between interior and exterior spaces.

Living area (top), eat-in kitchen (bottom)

Maisonette with rooftop garden retreat

Schöneberg
10781 Berlin

GFA 275 m²
GV 950 m³

ZappeArchitekten
www.zappearchitekten.de

Client: private

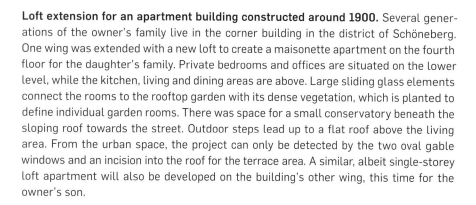

Terrace

View from the street

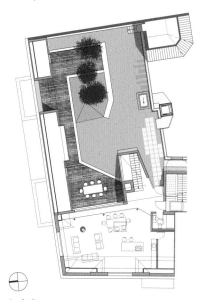

Loft floor plan

Loft extension for an apartment building constructed around 1900. Several generations of the owner's family live in the corner building in the district of Schöneberg. One wing was extended with a new loft to create a maisonette apartment on the fourth floor for the daughter's family. Private bedrooms and offices are situated on the lower level, while the kitchen, living and dining areas are above. Large sliding glass elements connect the rooms to the rooftop garden with its dense vegetation, which is planted to define individual garden rooms. There was space for a small conservatory beneath the sloping roof towards the street. Outdoor steps lead up to a flat roof above the living area. From the urban space, the project can only be detected by the two oval gable windows and an incision into the roof for the terrace area. A similar, albeit single-storey loft apartment will also be developed on the building's other wing, this time for the owner's son.

Rooftop garden with conservatory and outdoor steps (top), kitchen and living area (bottom)

Filling the gap

Dunckerstrasse 2a
10437 Berlin

GFA 1,275 m²
GV 3,500 m³

CKRS-Architektengesellschaft mbH
www.ckrs-architekten.de

Client: private

Maisonette

Staircase

Plan

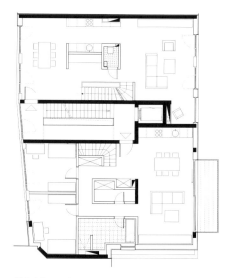

Third floor plan

New development of an apartment building with a commercial unit. The garden house in the district of Prenzlauer Berg closes a war-induced gap in the local *Gründerzeit* architecture, taking current housing and living requirements into account: on one side of the staircase, two maisonette apartments are positioned one above the other, with four and five rooms respectively – one with a garden, the other with a rooftop terrace. The other side is occupied by a commercial unit and three apartments above it, each with two to four rooms respectively. The five apartments are largely barrier-free. Their floor plans develop around inserted cores. The resulting ability to walk in a circle around the apartments picks up on traditions of Berlin bourgeois floor plans. To keep the construction period as short and quiet as possible, the load-bearing elements were assembled on-site out of semi-prefabricated reinforced steel units. The exterior walls are timber frame constructions with a curtain-wall façade made of fibre cement boards.

View from the front courtyard (top), apartment towards the rear courtyard (bottom)

Ado 21 – Pro Maxx

| Adolfstrasse 21 | GFA 2,025 m² | **hmp hertfelder – montojo planungsgesellschaft mbh** | Client: Pro Maxx gGmbH |
| 13347 Berlin | GV 6,100 m³ | www.hertfelder-montojo.de | |

Fourth floor plan

Apartment

New construction of an apartment building with a day care centre and consulting rooms. The property's owner is a social institution that provides housing for mothers with children and young people's cohabitation in pre-war housing. The new development fills the gap in the street's row of housing due to wartime damage. The project was developed with a district cooperative: to enable the construction of a day care centre, offices and consulting rooms for the social institution on the two lower levels, 13 age-appropriate owner-occupied apartments were built on the levels above, since these are lacking in the neighbourhood. Although their buyers thereby co-financed the social facilities, the owner-occupied apartments are still in the lower price segment: early coordination between all participants and especially cost-conscious planning for the building methods, standards and equipment kept the building costs at an extremely low level.

Living by Frankfurter Tor

Warschauer Strasse 5–8
Frankfurter Tor 8a
10243 Berlin

GFA 25,700 m²
GV 89,000 m³

GBP Architekten GmbH
www.gbp-architekten.de

Client: Cresco Capital Group

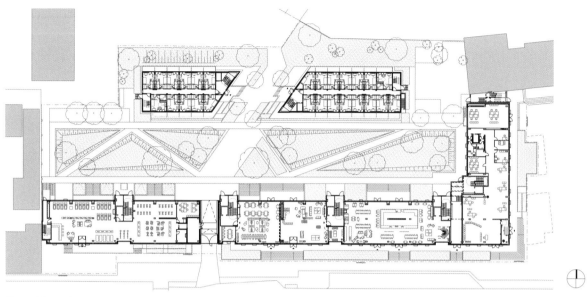

Ground floor plan

Lobby for students

Façade facing the street

Conversion and extension of an office complex built in 1974. The two-winged pre-fabricated, reinforced concrete building was completely gutted and given staggered floors. Two new rear houses have been constructed in the inner courtyard. A total of 567 apartments, including 485 student flats with kitchenettes and bathrooms were developed in this way with sizes of 18 to 24 square metres, as well as 82 micro-apartments with 25 to 39 square metres' space. Gastronomic and commercial areas are situated on the ground floor. The students' lobby is a central meeting place, providing space for cooperative concepts and flexible use. The ensemble adjoins with the preservation-listed development by Hermann Henselmann along Karl-Marx-Allee and Frankfurter Allee. Green elements on the new façade refer to their copper domes. The transoms of the new windows are also inspired by the neighbouring towers.

View from the courtyard (top), micro-apartment and student's flat (bottom)

Schlüterstrasse

Schlüterstrasse 40
10707 Berlin

GFA 5,625 m²
GV 22,680 m³

Axthelm Rolvien Architekten GmbH
www.axthelm-rolvien.de

Client: private

Garden house

Plan

New housing and commercial development. The building is situated in a side street of Kurfürstendamm. The courtyard garden connects the seven-storey front building to the four-storey rear section. The façade facing the street is aligned with the preservation-listed neighbouring buildings. It assumes their height as well as their typical projections and structures, but also gives them a contemporary appearance. White slab bands protrude between the room-high glass fronts. The lower levels are used commercially as shops and offices. The apartments are accommodated on the upper floors. Both sections are topped by penthouse apartments with broad terraces.

View from the street (top), view from the garden house and kitchen (bottom)

Housing in Albrecht-Achilles-Strasse

Albrecht-Achilles-Strasse 65
10709 Berlin

GFA 7,975 m²
GV 26,975 m³

Stephan Höhne Gesellschaft von Architekten mbH
www.stephan-hoehne-architekten.de

Client: Kurfürstenlogen Wohnbau Berlin GmbH
represented by Baywobau Baubetreuung GmbH

View from the courtyard

New housing development. 61 apartments with sizes ranging from two to four rooms and 65 to 153 square metres are distributed over seven floors. The building is close to the Schaubühne theatre in a side street of Kurfürstendamm and replaces an inconspicuous post-war office building. The new development picks up on the design elements of listed buildings from the 1920s and 1930s that characterise the neighbourhood. The central building section withdraws from the street, allowing front flowerbed zones that are typical for the area. The flowerbeds and small private gardens in the courtyard provide even the mezzanine apartments with an exclusive living environment. The rear house, which is connected to the rear side of the existing row of housing, opens up on three sides towards the green courtyard. Three entrances provide access from the street, while the garden house is reached from inside the block.

View from the street with flowerbeds (top), standard floor plan and plan (bottom)

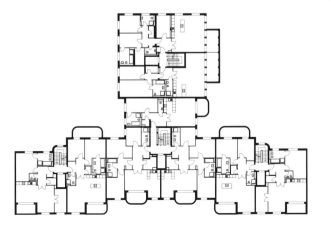

Minimal living

Prenzlauer Allee 7	GFA (new building)	3,500 m²	**NÄGELIARCHITEKTEN**	Client: private
10405 Berlin	GFA (existing building)	620 m²	**Gudrun Sack Walter Nägeli GbR**	
	GV (new building)	10,500 m³	www.naegeliarchitekten.de	
	GV (existing building)	1,550 m³		

View from the street

Bay window facing the street

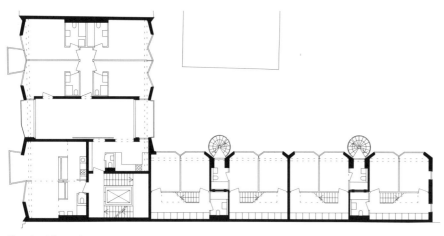

Standard floor plan

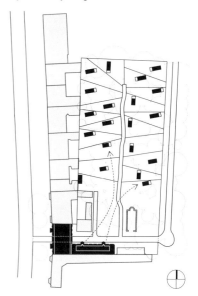

Plan with rear yard

New development for living, art and business in front of a firewall. The project on the site of a former cemetery was developed as a joint building venture and involved the users of the existing structures. The old buildings and remains from the time of the cemetery have been retained. Studios, exhibition spaces and offices are situated on the ground floor, while 25 small maisonette apartments are accommodated on the levels above. Wooden suspended ceilings allow them to be reconfigured depending on the user's living situation. An apartment can therefore be anything from a single 55-square-metre room with a gallery to three or even four rooms. To save space, the folded façade uses dry wall elements with special insulation. Although it is extremely thin, it provides very good noise and heat insulation. The building received "KfW-Effizienzhaus 55" certification and is supplied by a cogeneration unit. Winding stairs connect each of the apartments to one flexibly usable additional space in the yard behind the building.

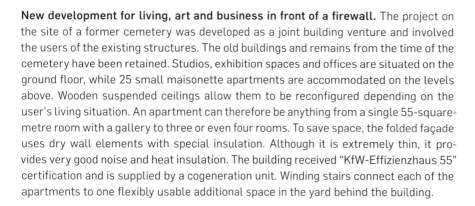

Side wing from the yard

Meubles à la Mies

Prenzlauer Allee 7
10405 Berlin

FA 200 m²

**wiewiorra hopp schwark
Gesellschaft von Architekten mbH**
www.whs-architekten.de

Client: private

View from the lounge area

Kitchen block worktop

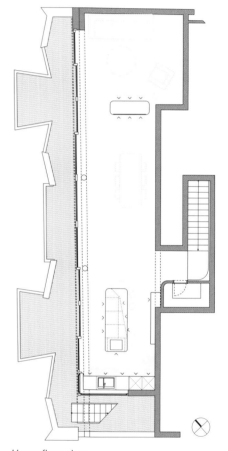

Upper floor plan

Fitted furniture for a penthouse apartment. The form and materials of the three pieces penetrate the simplicity of the cool modern interior. Finely grained rosewood and Brazilian natural stone in green and pink give the rooms a refined, patinised character. The furniture acts as a consistent design theme through the kitchen, living area and bedroom. The pieces stand freely in the open space like sculptural objects. Curved wooden elements wrap themselves around the edges, giving them the appearance of stones that have been rounded by water. The corners of the rectangular natural stone worktop in the kitchen are also rounded. The base recedes wherever one can sit at the kitchen block. One sibling piece of furniture divides the open living space into dining and lounge areas. The third piece structures the bedroom on the floor below. It is a wardrobe and also forms the back of the bed, thereby defining the way to the en-suite bathroom.

Kitchen (top), bedroom (bottom)

Q23 park-side housing

Hansestrasse 76–80
21337 Lüneburg

GFA 3,425 m²
GV 11,400 m³

q:arc Jakubeit & Rapp Partner Architekten mbB
www.qarc.de

Client: Sparkassen Hanse Immobilien GmbH

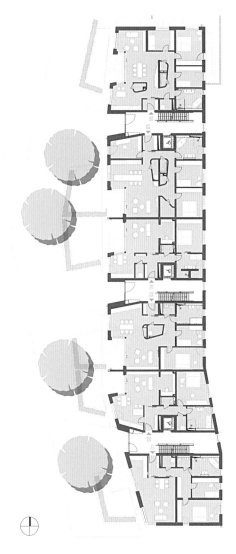

Ground floor plan

Hallway

Loggia facing the park

New development with 17 owner-occupied apartments and an underground car park following a competition in 2013. The house is part of the quarter known as the Hanseviertel, an urban expansion to the northeast of Lüneburg's centre that has been developed since 2010. It marks the eastern boundary of the new Stadtpark Hanseviertel. Projections and large loggias in the façade facing the park connect the building to the open space. The apartments have a size between 85 and 140 square metres, while the rooms are 2.7 metres high. The floor plans are flexibly designed. Each apartment has natural light from two or three sides. Three hallways provide barrier-free access to the apartments from the park. The building fulfils the "KfW Effizienzhaus 55" standard and received a Gold Certificate from the German Sustainable Building Council.

View from the park (top), apartment (bottom)

EFH_SAWI

| Gössweinsteiner Gang
14089 Berlin | GFA 150 m²
GV   470 m³ | **Claudius Pratsch _ studio für architekturen**
www.s-f-a.eu | Client: Prof. Dr. Karin Wilhelm, Johann Sauer |

Living area

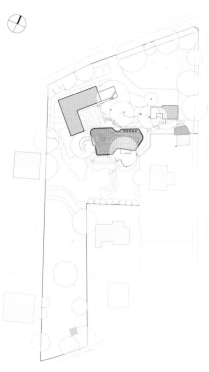

New construction of a single-family home. The single-storey building is inserted into a sloping property not far from the River Havel in a way that does not obstruct the view from the family's existing house. Between maple trees and a large lime tree, the curved green roof forms a new horizon in the natural topography. The shell construction consisting of prefabricated timber elements was erected in just under two weeks. The massive timber ceiling is supported by fine steel pillars. The bedrooms and kitchen are positioned towards the northwest. Together, the red-varnished plywood façade with a patio in front of it form the shielding back to the main building. A glass strip sets the roof apart from the façade below it. The living rooms flow into each other smoothly. They are situated in the southeast and open up through a room-high glass façade with three slatted elements facing a garden forecourt under the lime tree. The exterior grounds were designed by the office gm013 | giencke mattelig gbr bdla.

Plan

View from the southeast with the garden forecourt (top), view from the northwest with patio (bottom)

Waldhaus Pankow

Wackenbergstrasse 55
13156 Berlin

GFA 225 m²
GV 866 m³

Söllner Wagner Architekten PartG mbB
www.soellnerwagner-architekten.de

Client: private

View from the garden

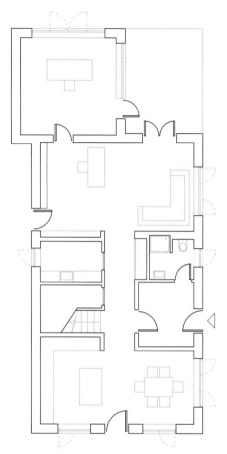

Ground floor plan

Plan

New construction of a single-family home using a wooden post and beam method.
The two-storey building with a flat studio extension towards the garden was erected on
a property with tall fir trees. The existing trees determined the orientation of the house.
Its southern gable faces the street. The new building's form and distribution is almost
archetypical, yet its colour and material contrast strongly with the neighbouring houses,
most of which were built in the 1930s. The house is clad in larch wood that has been
varnished in anthracite. The semi-open living area is situated on the ground floor, while
the upper level provides closed rooms for privacy. The house was built in accordance
with the "KfW-70 standard" – without using foil for the wall structure – and insulated
with wood fibres. The outward-opening wooden windows with triple insulating glass
were developed specially for the project.

View from the street (top), kitchen (bottom)

Two houses in Stechlin

Bahnhofsweg 5/5a · 16775 Stechlin

GFA 345 m² · GV 1,150 m³

mna merten nibbes architekten · www.mna.de

Clients: Rhein/Rehbein, Krebser/Koch

Living area, House R

Entrance, House R

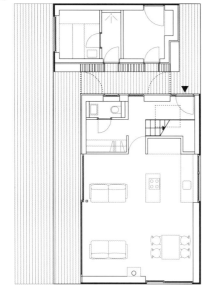

Ground floor plan, House K

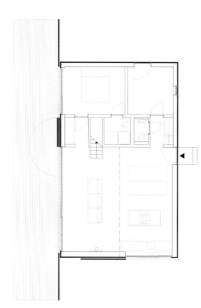

Ground floor plan, House R

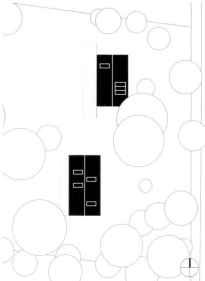

Plan

New development of two weekend houses. The buildings have offset positions to pick up on the structure of the village development, retain the existing pine trees and create protected exterior grounds. Both houses have the same profile, but different lengths and ground plans. The façades and roofs are clad in black-oiled larch wood. In the smaller House R, the entrance leads directly to a living room that is open all the way up to the roof ridge, which is naturally illuminated by a large skylight. The windows towards the garden span the entire width of the room. When their sliding shutters are open, they extend the rear wall of the garden terrace. In the larger House K, an open corridor on the ground floor separates the living and sauna areas. The corridor also connects the building's two loggias along its longitudinal sides, while serving as an exterior space for the sauna and as storage for firewood. In 2017, House K was awarded the Building Culture Prize of the Community of Gransee.

View from the north (top), garden side, House R, closed and open (bottom)

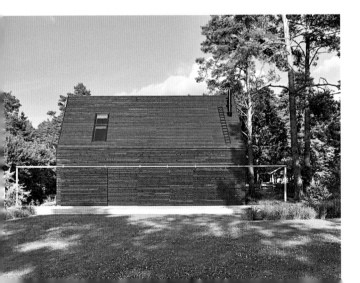

Urban barn

Palo Alto
California
(USA)

GFA 385 m²
GV 1,150 m³

Goderbauer Architects GmbH
www.goderbauer.com

Client: private

Gallery level

Ground floor plan

Shell construction with steel supports

Conversion of an early-20th century residential building. The client requested a simple house like a barn in downtown Palo Alto. The furniture and architecture of the Shakers and works by the concept artist Gordon Matta-Clark served as inspiration. Another requirement was to largely retain the existing form and envelope of the house. Thus, the window formats were softened into regular rectangles and the garden façade was recessed to create a covered exterior seating area. By contrast, the interior was completely gutted and the staircase was moved, converting the former eight rooms into a broad loft with a gallery level. Steel frames strengthen the load-bearing structure of the timber building. The building exterior is clad in cedar wood; a zinc roof that is typical for barns replaces the otherwise usual bitumen tiles. A homogenous coat of paint moderates the effect of the framework and ornamental details.

View from the southeast (top), living room from the veranda (bottom)

Water tower

Werderscher Damm 5
14471 Potsdam

GFA 185 m²
GV 470 m³

Wirth Alonso
www.wirth-alonso.de

Client: Katrin Wirth

View from the street

Renovation and conversion of a railway water tower into a holiday apartment. Built
in 1910 beside the station Kaiserbahnhof, it fell into decay after years of dereliction.
Although not formally preservation-listed, its location between Park Sanssouci and
Wildpark Potsdam means it is covered by UNESCO World Heritage regulations on pro-
tecting the surrounding areas. The tower's form and materiality remain preserved. Inside,
an open living landscape unfolds on six levels, or seven including the rooftop terrace.
The light fittings contrast with the red walls and the anthracite of the steel elements.
The levels have different room heights, lighting conditions, furniture and materiality.
The kitchen is accommodated beneath the brickwork dome on the ground floor. Above
it, bedrooms with bathrooms cover the next three levels. Beneath the former water
tank, one room keeps the tower's history alive. The tank itself serves as a living room.
A window in its riveted wall provides a view of the Wildpark.

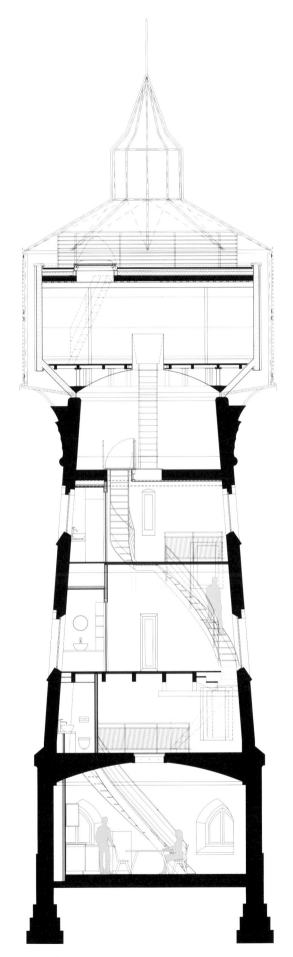

Section (left), rooftop terrace, living room, historical room, bedroom areas, kitchen (right, top to bottom)

Vesper house

Vor dem Schöneberger Tor 9	GFA 200 m²	**Frank Bohland Dipl.-Ing. Architekt**	Client: Frank Bohland
34369 Hofgeismar	GV 750 m³		

Staircase

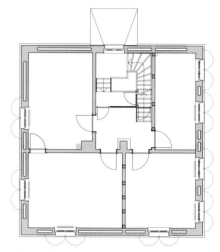

First floor plan

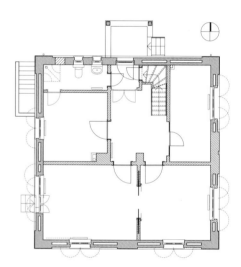

Ground floor plan

Renovation of a 1923 residential building according to preservation regulations.
The villa originally built in a "Heimatschutz" style was converted in 1971. The most
serious changes were reversed during renovation work. Wooden windows with historical divisions and transoms, replica shutters, a pergola and the garden's picket fence
revive the building's original condition. The walled-up windows on the southern façade
were reopened. Parts of the roof were newly covered with old materials. Inside, the still
existent case-lock doors were installed and the oak staircase refurbished. In a reconstruction measure, one room reveals the multicoloured loam paint, parts of which still
existed beneath the wallpaper. The cellar walls were sealed and the insulation for the
cellar ceilings and roof was enhanced. The original tile stoves could not be restored
and have been replaced by a contemporary heating system. The project was awarded
the DenkMalPreis monument-preservation award by the district of Kassel.

Condition in 2014

View from the street (top), living room (bottom)

Schönau house

Markt 10
Dom-Römer-Areal
60311 Frankfurt am Main

GFA 415 m²
GV 1,450 m³

von Ey Architektur
www.voney.de

Client: DomRömer GmbH

View from the street

Gable

New construction of a residential and commercial building following a competition in 2010. The aim of the Dom-Römer project was to resurrect an entire old town quarter through faithful reconstruction or, as in this case, with contemporary new buildings on historical plots. The building, which is only just over five metres wide, fills the gap left by a former half-timber house. Its façade is clad in slate. Pointed gables, floors projecting into the street and the red Main sandstone for the building base are additional references to the building's historical predecessor. The façade facing the street gains a new quality through its tripartite oriel windows and the interaction between sculptural forms and slate tiles. The exterior envelope recalls a tight-fitting sequined dress. Above the store on the ground floor, the four levels of a large apartment are arranged around the central atrium, as well as a terrace that has been inserted into the roof structure.

Stairs (top), floor plans (bottom)

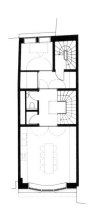

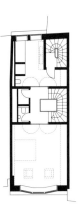
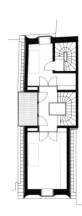

Classy and rough

Berlin's gastro-scene combines design and metropolitan flair

Restaurant Tim Raue in Berlin-Kreuzberg by Bruzkus Batek Architekten

The pressure has grown on Berlin's eating and drinking scene. Even for experienced night-crawlers, there is a vast number of newly opened establishments. The scene no longer just meets in bars and restaurants, but also at the numerous food festivals in the city, in the covered market in Kreuzberg known as Markthalle IX, around the Thai food stalls in Wilmersdorf's Preussenpark and in dinner clubs that operate by arrangement at semi-private locations. "The expectation is that there is always something new going on", the architect Ester Bruzkus explains. She and her long-standing office partner, Patrick Batek, have designed interiors for Tim Raue, Germany's most successful chef.

Tim Raue's reputation emanates from the rear courtyard: his main Berlin restaurant, which has been awarded two Michelin stars, is situated in a former gallery in Koch-strasse, Kreuzberg. Raue explicitly rejected a classic starred restaurant that looks like yesteryear Paris. The chef grew up in Kreuzberg, which is why the reference to the neighbourhood was so important to him. The entrance remains hidden and leads to a rear courtyard, as is typical for Kreuzberg. In the rooms, a group of artists have applied bright red, graffiti-like splashes of colour. Bruzkus and Batek chose an unusually plain style for the interior of a Michelin-starred restaurant. "Each one of Tim Raue's dishes is a piece of art", Ester Bruzkus declares. "We didn't want to steal his thunder with our design." The walnut tables and benches are their own designs, while the chairs stem from the Vitra collection. A few pieces of Asiatica are the only decoration, reflecting Raue's Asian-influenced cooking style. The reserved design is a radical break from the often opulent atmosphere of traditional gourmet temples.

The Tisk in Neukölln also presents a fine-dining concept without silver cutlery and white tablecloths. Guests look through the window front onto a tiled firewall full of graffiti, as in any corner bar. Clara Walter and Raphael Danke were not only responsible for the restaurant's design, but were also involved in selecting the cooking team. "So ultimately, the idea for the interior design merged with the cooking concept", Danke explains. The two designers chose the simple, natural materials of wood and stone. All wall and floor tiles are handcrafted and furnaced. The chairs and barstools were conceived by the internationally renowned designers Sam Hecht and Konstantin Grcic. They were produced in Italy by the manufacturer Mattiazzi, which stands for high-quality carpentry craftsmanship. "We don't work with industrial goods and, like the cuisine, prefer to use hand-produced ingredients", Danke explains.

GQ Bar in the Patrick Hellmann Schlosshotel, Berlin-Grunewald

The restaurant Ernst in Wedding is one of Berlin's most ambitious gastro-projects in recent years. It too receives its guests in a highly unconventional atmosphere. The office responsible for its design, Gonzales Haase AAS, clad the exterior façade in a simple, coarse grey plaster like a prefabricated housing estate. The entrance leads through a short, narrow corridor. The mirrored door with a doorbell is more reminiscent of a club than an expensive restaurant. In the 40-square-metre room, there is space for only twelve guests to enjoy the 26-course meal around the central cooking isle. The counter-like tabletop is made of maple, the walls of marble, while coarse plaster and concrete provide cladding. The glass for the ceiling lights is handblown and held by brass fittings. Like the cuisine, Gonzales Haase use materials in their raw condition, refining them into a sophisticated design menu.

From the outside, the Coda in Friedelstrasse, Neukölln also provides no indication that it is one of the most unusual gourmet locations in Berlin. The co-owner Oliver Bischoff is a trained product designer. His aim for the design is not only to address questions of style, but also to conceive holistic catering concepts: "I'm more likely to draw inspiration from an interesting article in the *Harvard Business Review* than from a designer magazine", he explains. Bischoff developed a fine-dining concept for the Coda in which everything focuses on desserts. He designed the lights and barstools himself. He also laid new flooring and planned the technical appliances used in the kitchen. The design and all building measures were planned down the smallest details. Compared to the quirky hipster style that is otherwise so prevalent in Neukölln, the Coda has a pure, avantgarde effect due to its orderly elegance.

The Coda and the Tisk are not just restaurants. Patrons can also simply enjoy an exciting cocktail at the bar. The boundaries between bar and restaurant have become fluent in Berlin, whereby bars are just as willing to experiment as the new eateries. Their drinks include mixtures with rare craft spirits and concoctions using rotary evaporators and vacuum sealers, emulating similar new techniques in cooking. However, it is the interior decoration that ultimately makes a bar a special place. "Guests in a bar want to dive into a different world", Thomas Karsten from studio karhard® explains. "That's why the design there must be more condensed." For the Neukölln speakeasy bar Truffle Pig, Karsten used materials with the haptic qualities of velvet and natural stone. The Truffle Pig offers plenty of atmosphere, for which elements such as lighting and acoustics are just as influential as the design. The architectural office that Karsten and his partner Alexandra Erhard founded in 2003 supervised all structural measures for Berlin's famous dance venue Berghain and its Panorama Bar. "Many aspects of the Berghain and its Panorama Bar were functional since people also dance there", Karsten explains. "We basically had the task of implementing as little design as possible." After all, Berlin's nightlife is world-famous for its anti-design attitude. The rough underground style that emerged in Berlin during the 1990s has not completely disappeared from the Truffle Pig, but is staged in a much more subtle and complex way.

Berlin's new concept-gastronomy scene is characterised by material and stylistic purity. Furthermore, as is the case with Tim Raue, the Ernst and the Tisk, there are always very strong references to the location. In the bars of major hotel chains, one finds the opposite trend: the Grand Hyatt at Potsdamer Platz presents the Jamboree, a bar that revives the flamboyant style of the 1980s. Instead of using a designer or architect from Berlin, it was developed by the London agency The Ghost Group, which specialises in gastro-concepts. The bar attracts an international clientele and could easily be found in one of the chain's other hotels in Shanghai or Dubai.

In the Schlosshotel in Berlin-Grunewald, which has now been renamed the Patrick Hellmann Schlosshotel to align it with the fashion brand of the same name, the men's magazine *GQ* offers its guests a "brand experience" in its own bar. Its massive coffered ceilings are framed by jagged-patterned wallpaper and wild, striped carpets. The choice of textile, marble and leather materials is expensive and refined. The style recalls London dining rooms such as the Bronte, designed by Tom Dixon, or the Park Chinois, which was created by the Paris designers Jacques Garcia and Alan Yau. The extravagant style of the new hotel bars hails the arrival of an opulent trend in Berlin that was hitherto more familiar in cities such as Paris and London. Inside these bars, the excessive, unfolding visuals reflect our omnipresent overstimulation by the media, advertising and consumption. It is all a far cry from the corner bar in Neukölln and the graffiti in Kreuzberg.

Truffle Pig in Berlin-Neukölln by studio karhard®

Flexim industrial estate

Boxberger Strasse 4	GFA 13,700 m²	**ZRS Architekten**	Client: Flexim GmbH
12681 Berlin	GV 52,800 m³	**Gesellschaft von Architekten mbH**	
		www.zrs.berlin	

Interior courtyard

Atrium with cafeteria

Third floor office

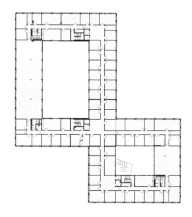

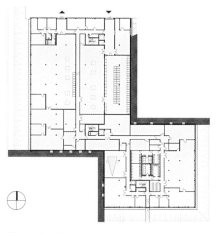

Floor plans: basement (bottom) and second floor (top)

New development for a company that produces ultrasonic flow meters. The corporate headquarters can be expanded to include further units to a maximum of 45,000 square metres. The courtyard concept with flexible spaces and common zones is guided by operative procedures. The building is a wood-concrete hybrid: the basement is made of reinforced concrete, as are the accessing cores, supports and binding joists on the three levels above. The ceiling boards consist of a wood-concrete composite. Apart from the accessing core, the top floor is a timber construction. The same applies to the vapour-permeable and climatically active building envelope. Its glazing, shading and nocturnal cooling elements ensure a pleasant climate throughout the year, with low energy requirements. Since regenerative energy sources are used (residual heat from communal sewage, heat pump, collectors and photovoltaics), the development consumes 30 percent less energy than EnEV regulations require.

View from the south (top), production line (bottom)

H.E.S. administrative building

Wolfgang-Küntscher-Strasse 18   GFA 2,475 m²   **Winking** · **Froh Architekten GmbH**   Client: H.E.S. Hennigsdorfer
16761 Hennigsdorf   GV   8,350 m³   www.winking-froh.de   Elektrostahlwerke GmbH

Foyer

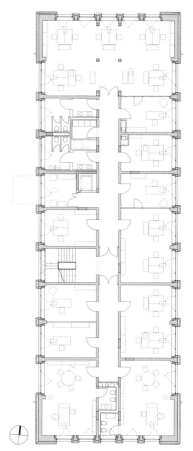

First floor plan

General overhaul of an office building erected in 1962. The three-storey building with a basement provides space for up to 100 administrative employees. New elements to its façade design translate characteristic aspects of early 20th-century industrial architecture into contemporary forms: the originally plastered façade of the brick building was insulated and received an attached brickwork envelope. The characteristic structure was preserved: parapets made of dark glass panels have replaced the former filler walls.

View from the south (top), office (bottom)

Office floor and entrance hall

Lietzenburger Strasse 44–46
10789 Berlin

GFA 1,125 m²
GV 3,125 m³

**platena+jagusch.architekten
Partnerschaftsgesellschaft mbB**
www.pja-berlin.de

Client: Polis Immobilien AG

Conference room

Meeting box

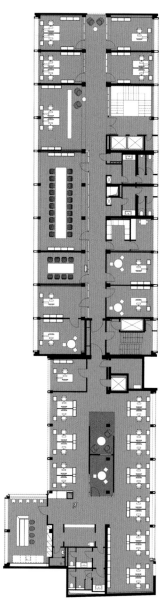

Office floor plan

New design of two areas in an office building from 1955. The office floor on the sixth storey is divided into a reception area with a conference section, a number of individual offices and an open zone. A box for meetings forms the centre of this open section. Another smaller box allows people to make undisturbed phone calls. The common room with a kitchen is situated in a bay towards the street. The raw reinforced concrete of the ribbed ceilings remains visible on the entire floor. It contrasts with the newly installed glass and aluminium fittings on the walls and ceilings. The entrance hall has regained its original size after a store that was installed at a later date was removed again. The reinforced concrete surfaces were also revealed to fully restore the design quality. The lift, a seating area and the bottom landings in front of the door are clad in concrete, thereby conforming with the surface of the 1955 steps.

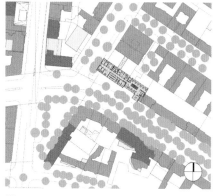

Plan

Entrance hall

Riemser Pharma, Greifswald location

Bahnhofstrasse 44b
17489 Greifswald

GFA 1,800 m²
GV 5,750 m³

**Reuter Schoger Architektur
Innenarchitektur Part mbB**
www.reuterschoger.de

Client: Riemser Pharma GmbH

Staircase in front of the cafeteria

Tea kitchen

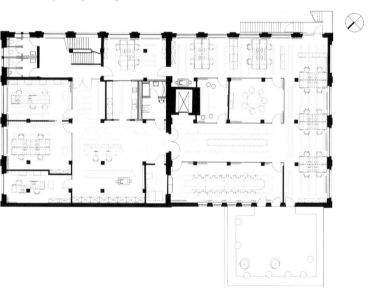

First floor plan

Conversion of a textile warehouse into office space. The former cloth warehouse was built in the 1950s and is situated near the railway station. The new interior finishing picks up on the aesthetics of the railway grounds, the coarse surfaces and powerful proportions of the building to create an open spatial effect with an industrial feel. A dark, polished poured-asphalt floor has elastic qualities that insulate impact noises and contrasts with the mould traces of the reinforced concrete ceilings. Seating furniture, ceiling areas, lights, tables, partitions and bar furniture each quote the capsule motif in their own way. It is a key element of the design and was already developed for the pharmaceutical company headquarters. The lighting design and an interplay between the existing structures and design responses combine to achieve inspiring placements – such as the ceiling elements in a capsule form.

Conference room

FULL NODE

Skalitzer Strasse 85
10997 Berlin

GFA 1,000 m²

LXSY Architekten
www.lxsy.de

Client: GNOSIS Service GmbH, All in Bits GmbH

Meeting box

Conference room

Office for four people

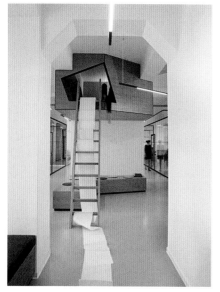

Snooze box

Conference room

Development of an office floor into a co-working space for blockchain businesses.
Blockchains are based on decentralised data processes. Thus the offices at FULL
NODE need no hierarchy. Crypto-traders, businesses and start-ups can network there
in a very simple and direct way. Open and protected rooms for almost every working
method support those activities. The fittings include fixed desks and offices, areas for
meetings, brainstorming, workshops and other events, lounges, phone booths, a café
and a snooze box. The rooms are situated in a preservation-listed post office built by
Jakob and Fritz Nissle in 1927. In this historical context, their equipment and design
provide a young, contemporary atmosphere that also fulfils current technical and
functional requirements.

Reception between event and café areas

Lounge

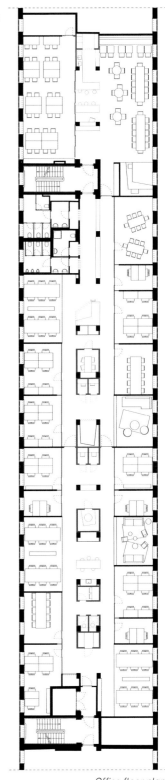

Office floor plan

Wikinghof – The light art of work

Erkelenzdamm 11/13	GFA (new building)	750 m²	**Vukovic + Rogulj**	Client: Akelius Erkelenzdamm GmbH
10999 Berlin	GFA (existing building)	11,200 m²	**Gesellschaft von Architekten mbH**	
	GV (new building)	2,850 m³		
	GV (existing building)	42,550 m³		

Library

Restaurant

Office

Office

Structural restoration, conversion and extension of a listed building by Kurt Berndt, erected in 1899. There are still apartments in the front extension built in 1912. The three industrial estates behind it are now used as the German headquarters of a Swedish housing company. The measures cleared retrofitted units out of the lofts and renovated and finished the entire building. In addition to accommodating 372 employees in individual spatial sequences, facilities include a restaurant, a gym, a sauna, a lounge, a library and a day care centre. Floating acoustic elements, selected lighting and furniture including specially designed pieces are all integrated into a design concept with Scandinavian-inspired natural material and colour accentuation, without hiding the character of the building, which is typical of Berlin and Kreuzberg.

Lounge (top), second courtyard (bottom)

taz new building

Friedrichstrasse 21	GFA 7,825 m²	**E2A Piet Eckert und Wim Eckert**	Client: taz, die tageszeitung.
10969 Berlin	GV 29,625 m³	**Architekten ETH BSA SIA AG**	Verlagsgenossenschaft eG
		www.e2a.ch	

Office

View of Besselpark

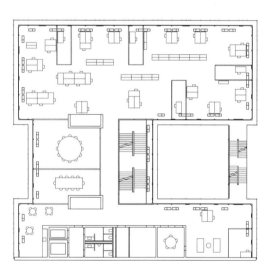

Fourth floor plan

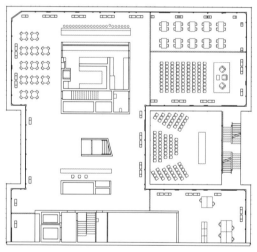

Ground floor plan

New development of an editorial and publishing house following a competition in 2014.
The corner building is part of a new media, art and creative quarter in the northwest of Kreuzberg. It mediates between the traditional block perimeter of Friedrichstrasse and nearby free-standing edifices from the time of the IBA '87. The publicly accessible ground floor includes a café, a shop and event rooms. The floor plans of the upper storeys are generally open and allow a wide range of different working methods. The architecture recalls the steel framework of the Moscow Shabolovka Radio Tower by Vladimir Shukhov, which was constructed in 1922. Its network structure achieved maximum load-bearing capacity using only few materials: all parts contribute equally and only achieve stability together. It is a system without hierarchy – and therefore both a constructive structure and an image of the organisation in one. From the outside, the networked structure presents itself as an intricate layer with French balconies.

View from the street (top), façade, exterior stairs on the eastern side, taz.panorama multifunctional room on the sixth floor (bottom)

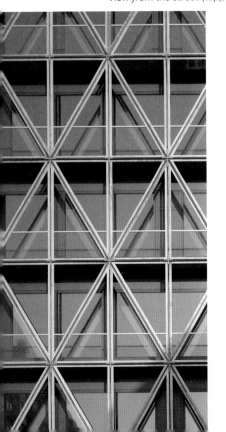

Vogtlandkreis district administration

Postplatz 5
08523 Plauen

GFA (new building)	6,400 m²
GFA (existing building)	15,400 m²
GV (new building)	24,850 m³
GV (existing building)	65,075 m³

BOLWIN WULF Architekten Partnerschaft mbB
www.bolwinwulf.de

Client: Vogtlandkreis District Administration

Old building at Postplatz

View from the northeast

Tea kitchen in the old building

Courtyard staircase corridor

Conversion and extension of a listed building for an administrative authority. The project was the result of a competition in 2009. The prestigious core of the local authority is formed by the former Tietz department store, which was built by Emil Rösler in 1912. It was renovated according to preservation regulations and is now the address, calling card and main entrance of the ensemble. On the rear side along Forststrasse, further buildings were renovated and supplemented by two new sections. A long interior courtyard, which is characterised by the rising terrain, runs through the complex. Other inner courtyards structure the buildings. A two-storey foyer acts as a hub at the heart of the ensemble. Inside, areas stemming from a wide range of periods create a variety of rooms, which are designed with according diversity.

Foyer (top), old and new building sections, plan (bottom)

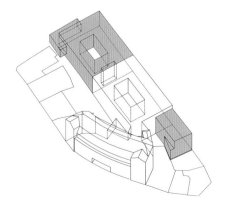

Supplementary building, Oranienburg tax authority

Heinrich-Grüber-Platz 3
16515 Oranienburg

GFA 3,325 m²
GV 12,050 m³

ARGE DeZwarteHond. | wiewiorra hopp schwark
Gesellschaft von Architekten mbH
www.whs-architekten.de

Client: Brandenburgischer Landesbetrieb
für Liegenschaften und Bauen (BLB)

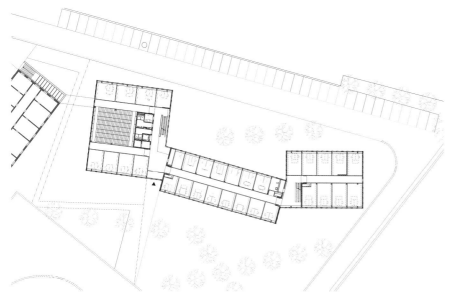

Ground floor plan

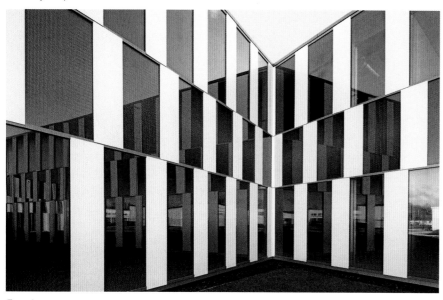

Façade

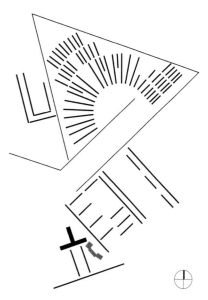

Plan

Extension for an authority. The main building of the Oranienburg Tax Authority was once the headquarters of the inspectorate for all concentration camps. The separate new building reflects the National Socialist past with a strictly autonomous design: it is dedicated to setting itself apart and makes no reference to the building used for criminal purposes. Neither the entrance nor the underground connection to the old building is visible. Instead, the central theme is an irritating façade band. The central band of the three window rows is slightly offset, creating an optical illusion known as the "café wall illusion": horizontal lines no longer appear to be parallel. It also remains unclear how many floors are hidden behind the façade (there are actually two). The building was built in the spirit of the Passive House standard. It was awarded a Silver Certificate by the Federal Assessment System for Sustainable Building.

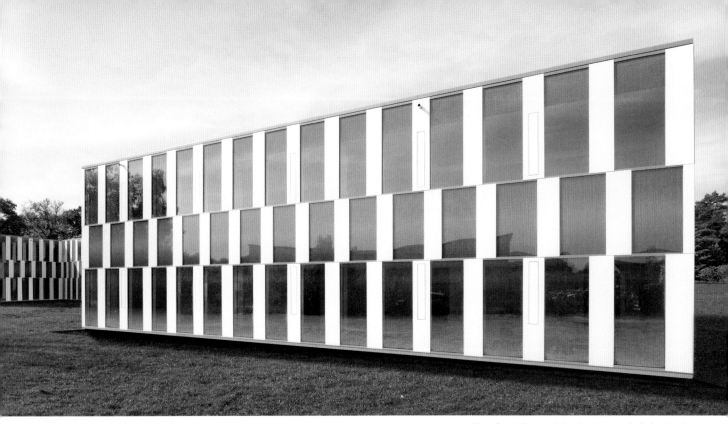

View from the north (top), entrance hall (bottom)

Greenland Central Plaza

Dongfeng East Road
450046 Zhengzhou
(China)

GFA   746,200 m²
Height 284 m

gmp · Architekten von Gerkan, Marg und Partner
www.gmp.de

Client: Zhongyuan Real Estate Business
Department of the Shanghai Greenland Group

Sky Lobby

Façades of tower and podium

Ground, 11th, 15th and 16th floor plans

New development of two high-rise buildings with separate podiums. The 63 floors of the Greenland Towers ascend into the sky of the Zhengzhou metropolis with its ten million inhabitants. Every eight floors, Sky Lobbies structure the silhouettes of the twin towers. These Sky Lobbies are public areas in the vertical plane that can be used in a wide range of ways – for instance as an outdoor terrace at an altitude of 240 metres. Each of the towers comprises 232,000 square metres. Their floor plans are offset around a rectangular building core like windmills. All offices are naturally ventilated using hidden apertures in the façade profiles. The eight-storey Sky Atrium near the top of the towers is reserved for exclusive uses: for instance as an event location for exhibitions and concerts. The three-storey Sky Commerce adjoins with the Atrium, providing restaurants, shops and a spa.

View from the east

Hampton by Hilton Berlin Alexanderplatz

| Otto-Braun-Strasse 69 | GFA 19,300 m² | **Collignon Architektur und Design GmbH** | Client: Lambert Wohnbau GmbH |
| 10178 Berlin | GV 66,550 m³ | www.collignonarchitektur.com | |

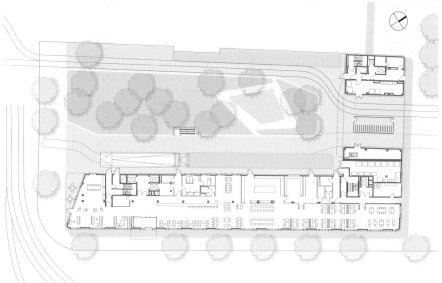

Ground floor plan

View from the south

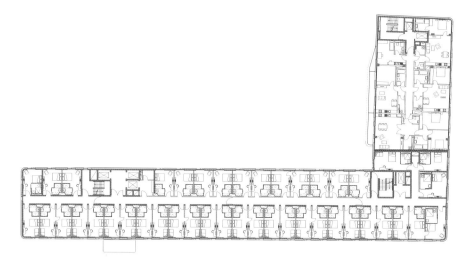

Standard floor plan

New development of a hotel and a residential building. The L-shaped nine-storey edifice assumes the scale of Socialist urban planning, but occupies the space along the block perimeter that was formerly used as a car park. The ground floor is largely glazed. The translucent façade above is defined by bands of perforated and mainly curved aluminium sheeting. Its profile recalls the waves of a curtain and gives the building its material lightness. At the same time, the panels provide shade and act as a parapet. The hotel's 344 rooms make it the world's largest Hilton establishment of its kind for the mid-price segment. The basement houses an underground car park with 27 parking spaces. The property was divided to create a new plot for the building along Mollstrasse, which now houses 40 new apartments. The largely green area behind the new building is a peaceful place for people in the neighbourhood.

View from the east (top), hotel façade detail (bottom)

Lenas am See restaurant

Seestrasse 10
86919 Utting am Ammersee

GFA 610 m²
GV 1,925 m³

Baldini Bleschke Architekten Partnerschaft mbB
www.baldinibleschke.de

Client: Lena Mielke, Lenas am See GmbH

Bar

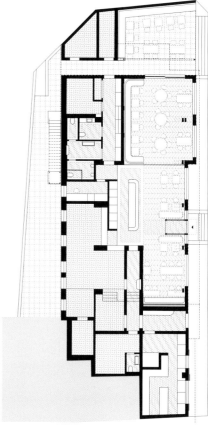

Ground floor plan

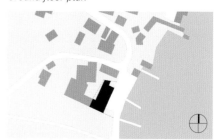

Plan

Conversion and renovation of a guesthouse. The building on the bank of the Ammersee was constructed in the early 20th century using a wooden post and beam method to serve as a boatyard warehouse. After the war, it was converted into a lakeside café. Over the years, the building, which is only used seasonally, fell into disrepair due to regular flooding damage. It was completely overhauled and restructured before being reopened as the restaurant Lenas am See. The entire load-bearing structure and all the building technology was renewed and the interior redesigned. The ground floor houses areas for guests, including an ice cream parlour and other terraces. A new loft apartment was built that overlooks the Ammersee and is accessed via outdoor stairs on the side facing away from the lake.

View from the lake (top), dining area (bottom)

Run over by yesterday

How urban is Berlin's inner-city motorway?

I am not too keen on cars, but I like Berlin's inner-urban motorway. When I get the chance to be a passenger in a car, I prefer the A 100. Rushing through tunnels, over bridges and along firewalls (often painted with completely out of date, faded advertising) has its appeal even to a passionate cyclist like me. From the outside, the city motorway also impresses in some places with its hyper-urban situations – for instance the nocturnal view from Kaiserdammbrücke onto the deep escarpment down to the archaically roaring traffic, with the Funkturm and the ICC in the background. The A 100 is more than just a thoroughfare, especially in places where the motorway and architecture were planned together: for instance beside the ICC, at the Bierpinsel or in Schlangenbader Strasse, where the housing was developed on top of the motorway. The latter two structures are by now preservation-listed, not only since they express a certain "westalgia", but also because they reveal a great deal about the period of their construction: the economic and social optimism, the desire for unlimited mobility in the confined West Berlin and the period when architects were apparently allowed to construct any designs, regardless how audacious they were.

Urban motorway at Bundesplatz (left),
brownfield meadow under Rudolf-Wissell-Brücke

However, in Germany, the land of the car manufacturer, hardly any planners dare to touch the areas along the A 100. Instead, there is a completely exaggerated and unwarranted respect for the car, as reflected in the land-use plans with strict functional distinctions, noise protection regulations, sound-barriers and triple-glazed windows. Wherever architecture has to take cars into account rather than the other way around, it is virtually impossible to conceive any better design along transport routes.

Automobiles are loud and dirty, not the concrete and steel that has been developed into a motorway. If cars soon get quieter, cleaner and slower, or other vehicles use the A 100, things might suddenly seem different. "Since the introduction of the 30 kph speed limit, we can sit and chat in front of our office", the Berlin architect Max Schwitalla explains. His office is situated in Leipziger Strasse. Schwitalla has already developed a number of ideas for transport-related spaces. He wants to replace street parking spaces with mini-houses, reactivate the railway known as the Siemensbahn to use it as a testing route for autonomous vehicles, and develop residual plot portions behind firewalls along the S-Bahn tracks.

By today's criteria, those redundant plots are unusable. They can also be found along the A 100, even where the development comes especially close to the motorway. For instance pedestrians can discover as yet untapped potential at Bundesplatz despite the urban density: embankments covered in trash, only half-developed properties and a sinister car park right by the A 100 that is also intended as a station forecourt. Why not integrate the parking space into a building there? Why not locate noisy or less residentially compatible uses such as workshops, small manufacturing businesses and clubs, which are increasingly being pushed out of *Gründerzeit* neighbourhoods, beneath the motorway? One successful example can be found in a structure erected in 1882: the arches of the Berlin S-Bahn, which are now used by stores and restaurants. As early as in 1996, the "Lemon" building design in Halensee by Hilde Léon and Konrad Wohlhage showed how particularly expressive architecture can be achieved on small residual plots beside the motorway. The office building's form and position have become its own advertisement.

I myself can get quite enthusiastic about living by the urban motorway – firstly because a major city also requires "poor" (i.e. somewhat louder, but also more affordable) residential areas if the centre is to remain populated. Secondly, in a city where so many

unconventional forms of living coexist, plenty of people deliberately seek unconventional neighbourhoods, where there is a certain metropolitan poetry in the roar of traffic and the flashing lights. (I live directly at Frankfurter Tor.)

There have been times when greater creativity was invested in integrating the A 100 into the city and accessing difficult spaces – for instance in June 1989, when the newly founded Architekturforum Aedes organised a workshop process to develop the Halensee freight railway station in response to considerations by the Senate to build around 1,400 apartments on a lid over the station. Although the fall of the Wall shortly afterwards briefly alleviated the densification pressure on West Berlin, the gallery exhibited the submitted designs in 1990. Some of them also covered the neighbouring A 100 or used it as a corridor for development.

Development beneath the highway by the Bierpinsel tower restaurant in Berlin-Steglitz

Occasionally, such ideas recall the audacious plans for the urban motorway in the 1970s, with its undeveloped (inner-urban) tangents. The plans represent the combined consideration of road and edifice construction, including auxiliary developments with shear high-rise tower façades, terraced housing over the motorway and green slopes over its junctions. Such Senate concepts, competition plans and student ideas can be found in a study published in 1980 by the later Senate Director of Building, Hans Stimmann from the Technische Universität Berlin. At the time, Stimmann, who would consistently call for the urban planning integration of developments over motorways, concluded as follows: "All projects to develop over motorways were either aimed at preserving the use value of already used adjoining areas, or improving the exchange value of areas intended for use [as a motorway]." He regarded the development ideas, "as a way of adding impetus to implementing motorway planning that had already been decided upon". As soon as resistance to the motorway was broken, its construction continued even without housing developments over it or any tunnel-building. Stimmann particularly regarded the housing over the motorway in Schlangenbader Strasse, which had just been completed at the time of publication, as a write-off project and an "economic, urban-planning and political failure" that was upheld because there was simply no way back.

Presumably one should do without developments over the motorway in future, if only because of the extensive structural and social management of major structures of this kind. However, the above-mentioned "Schlange" ("Snake") development is (once again) regarded as a good residential location. Ironically, the motorway stump at Schlangenbader Strasse, which has now been downgraded to a major urban road, would probably have been earmarked for demolition by now were there not the building on top of it. The housing development has become the justification for the road's existence, although the opposite was once the case. Strictly speaking, the Bierpinsel bridge further along the route has also become obsolete, were it not for the definitive restaurant tower.

However, it is likely that the actual urban motorway will continue to be needed as a thoroughfare, although one could reduce the space it occupies and make it more permeable. The A 100 separates the Tempelhofer Feld from the district of Tempelhof. The Schöneberg junction with its western tangential stump is simply superfluous as a four-leaf clover formation. And there is even plenty of potential space in the highly complex conglomeration of over- and underpasses at the Funkturm triangular junction, as a visit to the Avus services confirms (incidentally, its interior is absolutely worth seeing). There at the centre of the motorway knot, there is little else to see apart from trucks, coaches and plenty of spacing greenery. In 2017, recognising that all this

"Lemon" office building in Berlin-Halensee by léonwohlhage

can add up to a large amount of building land, the Architekten- und Ingenieurverein zu Berlin (AIV) announced a Schinkel Competition for ideas on those residual spaces. The fascinating students' ideas highlight how much density and urban character is possible even in such locations. Coincidentally, no less than 50 years earlier, the AIV focused on a similar task with respect to the Schöneberg junction.

Seoullo by MVRDV in the South Korean capital

Under Rudolf-Wissell-Brücke

In transport-planning reality, however, Berlin's inner-urban motorway continues to be built in a similar way to motorways everywhere else: the extension to Treptower Park, which is currently under construction, mainly runs through an open trough. Noise-barriers line the motorway access roads and exits. The planned replacement for the Rudolf-Wissell-Brücke also represents another opportunity for new ideas and gained ground. But the winning design, which seems to have had the main aim of a smooth new construction without interrupting the traffic, now even plans two bridges. Not even the simple aesthetics of the bridge piers (simple double angles) can rival the dynamic, folded H-piers of the existing structure, although so many impressive design ideas have recently been implemented in the field of bridge building. In the meantime, the district of Charlottenburg-Wilmersdorf has expressed the desire to reroute the motorway over the S-Bahn ring railway track, with another branch further east over the River Spree. More than 20 hectares would be freed up in this way. Another example is the Funkturm triangular junction, which is soon to be modernised and represents an opportunity to reclaim space for the city and remove partitions. The district envisages a similar park to the one at Gleisdreieck and the desire for secondary effects is absolutely legitimate, considering the estimated investment costs of € 250 million over a planning period of seven years.

It is no doubt sensible to regard modernisation as motivation to correct the current situation, but the A 100 is hardly reconsidered in any fundamental way. Often it only takes a change of

perspective, as in 2010 in the Ruhr region (which was a European Cultural Capital at the time). The "Ruhrschnellweg" motorway was used for all kinds of activities, just not for cars. In Berlin, parts of the inner-urban motorway are used by the annual cycling demonstration known as the "Sternfahrt". If only that were possible more often! The climate economist Felix Creutzig from the Technische Universität Berlin, who specialises in cities and their transport systems, proposes one car-free Sunday a month on the A 100 as the basis for discussion. On the Minhocão elevated highway in São Paulo, the rule applies every Sunday and in the evenings for noise-pollution reasons. Creutzig believes it is by no means certain that the urban motorway is actually required to its present extent. Statistics on how and when the inner-urban motorway is used do not exist. "So we need to propose ideas, test what works and see where the traffic flows are diverted." Creutzig believes it is possible to use the A 100 in time slots for different modes of transport or exclusively for bicycles and buses: "The car takes a great deal of space. Other modes of transport can transport more people using the same space."

Elsewhere, policy and planning measures are less reserved in simply taking space away from cars: in Bogotá, a 24-kilometre highway for cyclists was created straight through the city. Paris has replaced riverside roads along the Seine with promenades and urban beaches. Furthermore, the office MVRDV transformed an elevated highway in Seoul into a green pedestrian zone. So the thoroughfare itself is not the problem – only its use.

Multi-storey car park under Joachim-Tiburtius-Brücke in Berlin-Steglitz

However, if one categorically refuses to reduce the space allocated to cars, developing over that space by covering it appears to be the simplest solution. Sankt Gallen has done that for a trade-fair hall, while Hamburg has implemented noise-protection measures in this way to the north of the Elbtunnel, thereby creating new green spaces. In Madrid the regained access to the Río Manzanares involved 56 kilometres of motorway and access roads, including entire motorway junctions, disappearing beneath new green areas – at a cost of over € 4 billion. Downtown Boston's sinking of its Central Artery has also reaped urban planning rewards. But was the so-called "Big Dig", which went far beyond the tunnelling measures for a few kilometres of highway, really worth the 25-year planning and construction period, including several construction scandals and costs of $ 14.6 billion?

In view of such sums to correct the car-compatible city, Berlin should seriously reconsider any further extension to the A 100. Everywhere else around the world, urban motorways are currently being demolished, converted or moved – and certainly not newly constructed. But in any case, perhaps Madrid and Boston are not the right role models for Berlin, a city that is critical of megaprojects. It may be simpler to use small measures and encourage the transport turnaround to succeed in a simpler, faster and cheaper way. Think of the creative energy that would be released if traffic suddenly became slower, quieter, cleaner, less voluminous and simply different!? I can see it before me: the urban motorway that is no longer a rear side, but a front side, where wind turbines rotate, on which bicycles and buses can travel and even pedestrians stroll. That is why Max Schwitalla calls for the "renegotiation of spaces intended for mobility in cities, in which more can be achieved than simply green areas along transport routes". Perhaps people will then live and work much closer to the A 100 than is the case today. Workshops, stores, multi-storey bicycle parking facilities and energy-storage could be built beneath it and houses erected on top of it. It would turn the urban motorway into one that truly stresses its "urban" nature.

Olympiapark Berlin depot

Prinz-Friedrich-Karl-Weg
14053 Berlin

GFA 1,750 m²
GV 9,100 m³

**TRU Architekten Töpfer, Bertuleit, Ruf, Lingens,
Bauerfeind, v. Wedemeyer Partnerschaft mbB**
www.truarchitekten.de

Client: Senatsverwaltung für Stadtentwicklung
und Wohnen

View from the rear

Hall

Plan

New construction of a personnel building and a hall. These are the first modules of
a central depot on the preservation-listed Olympic grounds. The warehouse, workshops
and common rooms were distributed around the grounds, mostly in later, non-listed
functional buildings. The new depot is embedded behind bushes at the edge of the park
by the Deutsche Sportforum. It will be extended by three additional halls. A broad can-
opy will connect all modules. The column-free halls are steel structures that allow
flexible uses and spatial division. They are naturally lit by a crown of skylights and
from the front through glazed sectional gates. The personnel building is a timber construction that houses offices, training rooms, changing rooms and sanitary facilities.
The façades are clad in wooden boards that have been varnished in several different
pre-weathering tones, which will gradually disappear as the natural weathering process
takes over.

View from the east (top), entrance area with stairs in the personnel building (bottom)

Ortenau bridge

Junction between	Length	290 m	**Henchion Reuter / EiSat GmbH**	Client: Landesgartenschau Lahr 2018 GmbH
B 3 and B 415	Height	50 m	**(Eisenloffel.Sattler + Partner)**	
77933 Lahr/Schwarzwald	Usable width	3.5 m	www.henchion-reuter.de	
			www.eisat.de	

Pylon

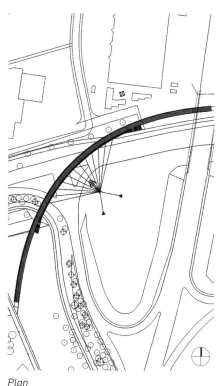

Plan

New construction of a pedestrian and cycle bridge. The project is the result of a competition in 2012. The bridge over the junction area of two national roads connects the Bürgerpark Mauerfeld and the Seepark Stegmatten. It became a landmark of the 2018 State Garden Show. Visible from afar, the sculptural pylon marks the junction and with it the entrance to the city. The bridge's broad curve is organised in three structurally independent zones: two ascents in conventional solid structures frame a fine steel configuration at the centre. Built as a cable-stayed bridge, the central section has a span of 115 metres, representing the actual main load-bearing structure. Its light, steel superstructure is diagonally suspended from a pylon using a system of cables and anchored within the traffic isle.

Access from the Seepark (top), view from the west (bottom)

Belvedere Würzburg

Hublandpark   GFA   670 m²
97074 Würzburg   GV   2,070 m³

SAUERZAPFE ARCHITEKTEN
www.sauerzapfearchitekten.de

Client: Landesgartenschau Würzburg 2018 GmbH

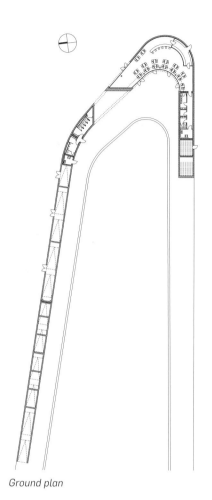

Ground plan

New development of a viewing structure for the Hublandpark following a competition in 2012. The promenade roof of the Belvedere is part of the Beltwalk in the new park. At the highest point of the tour, the structure provides a view of the terrain that was used for the Bavarian State Garden Show in 2018. There are storage rooms, a public toilet and a gathering space with a café inside the structure. A staircase leads up one side, while a barrier-free ramp provides access to the rooftop terrace from the other end. The developed areas of the reinforced concrete building are insulated from the inside. Visual concrete elements were painted black and hammered at lower levels. Refining the surfaces in this way is aimed at achieving more widespread acceptance of fair-faced concrete as a material.

→ Project 55 on page 148/149 for landscape architecture

View from the west (top) and the northeast (bottom)

Concrete garden house

Industriestrasse 1 79206 Breisach- Niederrimsingen	GFA 7 m² GV 20 m³	**Adrian Birkenmeier, freelance architect**	Client: Birkenmeier Stein + Design GmbH

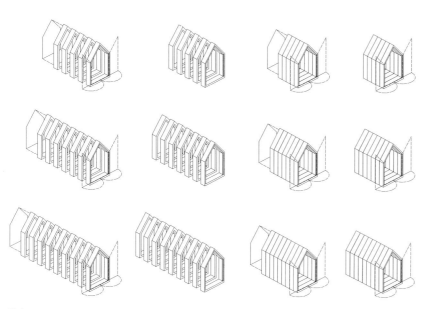

Scheme

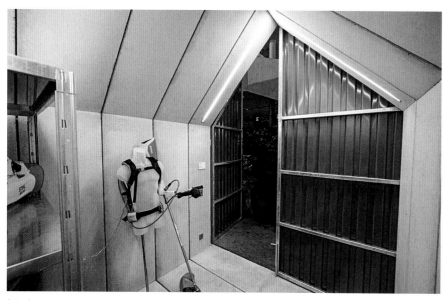

Interior

Prototype of a flexibly usable auxiliary building. A repeated element creates the original form of a house: the prefabricated reinforced concrete element comprises the roof, walls and floor plate all in one. It is produced in a form and moulding process and can be combined with any number of other such units. The result is a homogenous building with butt joints that are hardly visible. Builders can assemble the structure on-site, which takes less than half a day. The process involves placing the elements on strip foundations and screwing them together laterally. It is very easy to move the building at a later date. The building is durable and resistant to the weather, humidity and vandalism, making it suitable for use in public spaces.

Segment structure (top), colours and varieties (bottom)

Unprofitable?

Historical sports locations are a matter of concern
for preservation authorities

Many renowned architects have designed sports facilities in Berlin that we can now call historical and are preservation-listed: Fred Forbát, Hans Hertlein, naturally Ludwig Hoffmann, Jean Krämer, Otto and Werner March, Martin Wagner and, after the war, Selman Selmanagić and Ludwig Leo. Today, it is safe to say that such buildings are cause for concern in both the Senate and district councils. Like all monuments, they need to be maintained from time to time, but two aspects cause problems: the way the sports facilities are used has significantly changed in most disciplines, with repercussions for the structures themselves. Secondly, most sports facilities are gathering places where security and building standards have been drastically increased.

One instructive example is the Olympiapark, where all the problem areas can be studied on the basis of a wide range of sports facilities. They start with the small tennis stadium in Sportforumstrasse, which hardly anyone knows about because it in effect acts as a hidden children's playground. Trees have long been growing on its natural grandstand. A stone's throw away, the Haus des Deutschen Sports was inaccessible for decades behind the fence of the British military grounds. The strict, imposing, clearly National Socialist architecture has certainly lost its imperious effect. One can assume the buildings that once represented the Third Reich have no influence on the spirit of the Poelchau School for the future sports elite. The football club Hertha BSC and various other users also radiate a friendly aura. The Sportforum's indoor and open-air pools are well frequented, but the impressive domed hall is a greater concern due to its renovation requirements. It is currently used as a venue for budding rhythmic gymnasts and fencers. Cultural events are also planned for the characteristic domed hall once it has been renovated.

The small park used by a riding club is called Lindeneck. Its landscape has a certain attraction, which is equally true of the Olympic Equestrian Stadium. The Berlin Show Jumping Championships are held there, but apparently that is no reason for the Senate to go ahead with the long-awaited renovation measures.

The Olympic Stadium itself was converted for the 2006 FIFA World Cup by gmp Architects von Gerkan, Marg and Partners in both an agreeable and preservation-compatible way at a cost of € 242 million. One could call it a blessing, were it not for the fact that Hertha BSC has realised that the team has a competitive disadvantage in the spread-out, often sparsely filled Olympic Stadium.

Experience has shown that a much more intense football atmosphere is achieved in a compact stadium designed purely for football, with steeper stands and no racetrack between the pitch and the fans. The club now wants to build such an arena at the eastern end of the Olympiapark between Rominter Allee and Sportforumstrasse. The area

Domed hall of the Haus des Deutschen Sports at the Olympic site (left), Olympic Stadium

Finish line judge's tower, Karlshorst trotting racecourse

in the direct vicinity of the underground station is currently covered by a stretch of forest. Some residential and official buildings from the period of British occupation would have to be demolished and development work would affect the (currently interrupted) axis of Sportforumstrasse. The same applies to part of an adjoining playing field, known as the Schenkendorffplatz. The garden preservation authority is resisting the latter, since the Olympiapark is listed as cultural heritage. Such peripheral measures could be regarded as marginal compared to other building "sins" committed on the grounds. Perhaps one could conceive architecture for the new stadium that would fulfil the demands of the location in terms of its style and expression. At any rate the site at Hertha's headquarters, with its sporting surroundings, the image of the location and its transport connections are all ideal. So the debate on a new venue is in full swing.

The Olympic Swimming Pool at the northern end of the Olympic Stadium is a wonderful facility and a popular venue for swimming and diving. The latter discipline received a new 10-metre tower with a lift for the 1978 World Championships. However, this well-integrated measure made it necessary to sacrifice the original tower. Regular references are made to the substantial sums required to improve the swimming facility, most recently in 2016 when the pool was renovated.

Often, redundant grandstands are the most challenging problem for monument preservation authorities with respect to historical sports facilities, as is the case with the Olympic Pool, since they are seen to generate "uneconomic" operative costs. The Avus grandstand is a perfect example of the problem. It was built by Fritz Wilms for motor racing spectators in 1936. Although undoubtedly a monument, it has nevertheless been slowly decaying before the eyes of thousands of passing drivers every day, since the Avus is now used as a motorway. The only measures taken are the occasional removal of ruderal vegetation for safety reasons. Now, an investor intends to renovate the structure by the 100th anniversary of the Avus in 2021. But how do you use such a grandstand? The new owner has managed to gain approval from preservation authorities to install a glass platform and individual glass boxes on the stands for exhibitions and events. Offices, shops and perhaps a small Avus museum are planned for the rear side along Messedamm.

The Olympic Pool, the Wannsee lido and the historical indoor swimming baths are all structures to which residents feel an attachment on two different emotional levels. They are both a piece of local "homeland" culture and places of physical well-being. That in itself may warrant the cost of reconstructing and enhancing them in a way that respects preservation demands.

But districts have not always been able to fund their own building measures. It was possible to renovate the municipal baths in Kreuzberg (built in 1901), Spandau (1911), Neukölln (1914), Mitte (1930) and Schöneberg (1930) and adapt the facilities to today's requirements. However, other swimming venues such as the Wedding municipal baths were closed and demolished, or are currently empty. For instance, the plug was finally pulled on the 110-year-old Stadtbad Steglitz in 2002. Since then, there have only been temporary cultural uses and decay, although some students have since submitted revitalisation proposals. The owner, Berliner Immobilienmanagement GmbH, has put plans on hold. The situation is similar for the Hubertusbad in Lichtenberg, affectionately known as the "Hupe", which is 20 years younger than its Steglitz counterpart, but was also closed in 1991 due to technical deficiencies. Since then, all efforts to revitalise the stately Expressionist building have failed in view of the enormous funding requirements of around € 30 million. Since May 2018, there has been talk of "activation use", with "low-barrier interim utilisation by cultural actors and creative artists". That does not sound like reopening the public baths.

However, such a project was successful for the Stadtbad Oderberger Strasse, the former Volksbad Prenzlauer Berg, which had been empty since 1986. The impressive building by Ludwig Hoffmann was erected in 1902 in the form of a Renaissance palace. Now it has been revitalised and combined with an international language school and a hotel, while respecting monument preservation demands. Thus it is at least open to the general public to a limited extent.

The underlying problem of the bathing facilities from the period when Ludwig Hoffmann was Director of Municipal Building is their limited suitability for today's swimming sports and also leisure-orientated bathing, making their economically viable preservation difficult. The high air temperature and humidity, plus hygiene requirements, represent a great challenge to the old masonry. Dozens of small tubs and shower facilities are no longer required. Instead, spa, fitness and catering services are in demand. Thus it has become impossible to continue to operate some highly attractive, historical public baths, despite their listed status.

While sports halls and preservation-listed stadiums will always be usable in some contemporary form or other if they are appropriately equipped, Berlin's horse-racing courses are an especially endangered species. The enormous costs of the expansive grounds conflict with the declining popularity of gallop and trotting races. Of the nine originally existent Berlin horse-racing facilities, including the Rennbahn Grunewald on today's Olympiapark grounds, only two still operate today: Karlshorst and the Mariendorf trotting racecourse. They are joined by Hoppegarten

just outside the city limits. Preserving those few historical structures is the least of the problems when the institutions themselves are endangered. As is the case for most sports facilities, public funds are essential for their survival. Ultimately, the efforts are rewarding since the aim is to preserve not only the building culture, but also our socio-cultural heritage, as well as encouraging sports to improve public health.

Avus grandstand

Stadtbad Mitte

Moorhof

Nettgendorfer Strasse 7   GFA 350 m²   **PERACKIS.ARCHITEKTEN**   Client: Dr. Detlev Löchel, Sonja Stenzel
14947 Dobbrikow   GV 1,825 m³   www.perackis.de

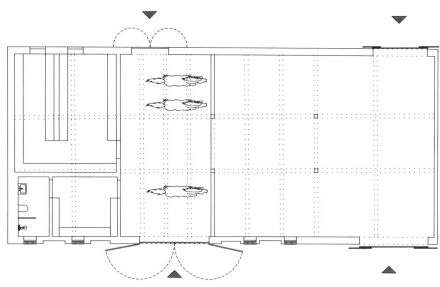

Floor plan

Plan of the four-sided farmyard

Renovated masonry with a new gate

Renovation of a barn with a riding stable for Icelandic horses. The building was erected
in 1890 and is one of four free-standing structures on a four-sided farmyard. The farm
is situated in a Brandenburg village in the Nuthe-Urstrom valley. Behind the barn, there
are wide-open fields and pastures for horses. The historical building is not preservation-listed, but has been restored as far as possible to its historical condition on the
request of the client to regain its original character. The solid masonry facing the yard
and the timber framework at the gables and facing the meadows have remained visible. New larch gates have replaced the former trapezoid sheet metal doors. Further
plans exist to renovate the house in future building measures and also to convert the
gatehouse for residential purposes. Holiday apartments are planned for the stable
buildings flanking the yard.

View from the yard (top) and from the meadow (bottom)

Tropical Balinese greenhouse

Gärten der Welt
Eisenacher Strasse 100
12685 Berlin

GFA 2,075 m²
GV 25,025 m³

HAAS | Architekten BDA
www.haas-architekten.de

Client: Grün Berlin GmbH

Interior

Façade heating

Façade section

New show greenhouse for the Balinese Garden at the Gardens of the World (Gärten der Welt). Until now, it had been accommodated in a heated greenhouse that was too small. The new hall was built around the existing structure, which was only then dismantled in order to protect the flora. The plants now have much more space in which to grow. A cold building forms an antechamber to expand the range of exhibits. Visitors can now enjoy an information area with a terrace to the west. The primary structure and envelope are modest. This allows the plants to take centre stage in the 40 by 50 metre, almost support-free hall and the Balinese atmosphere does not need to compete with any ornamental architecture. Innovative façade heating ensures the building is warm: the entire steel structure is filled with water at a temperature of 42 degrees. That is sensible from an energy perspective, since the building can be operated as a low-temperature system in this way.

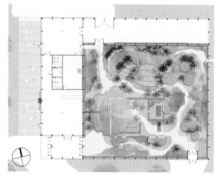

Ground plan

View from the east (top), tropical greenhouse (bottom)

Köpenick hospice | DRK Kliniken Berlin

Haus 27 Salvador-Allende-Strasse 2–8 12559 Berlin	GFA 1,300 m² GV 5,800 m³	**Heinle, Wischer und Partner, Freie Architekten** www.heinlewischerpartner.de	Client: DRK Kliniken Berlin	Köpenick, Gemeinnützige Krankenhaus GmbH DRK Schwesternschaft Berlin

Floor plan

View from the east

Interior courtyard

Communal area with kitchen

Main entrance

View from the north

New construction of a residential and nursing facility. The patients receive medical treatment there during the last days of their lives. At the same time, the surroundings must be made as pleasant as possible during that time and patients must have the opportunity to deal with personal issues in close contact with their loved ones. To that aim, the building is a nursing centre, apartment, meeting place, communication area and retreat, all at once. Each of the barrier-free single bedrooms has its own terrace with moveable elements made of wooden slats that can create a private space for every patient. The rooms are grouped around the central communal area and a shielded interior courtyard where guests, loved ones and care personnel can come together. For the sake of sustainable building, the hospice was built using timber frames with load-bearing exterior and interior walls.

View from the northwest (top), single bedroom (bottom)

Déjà vu

Berlin's school-building campaign is not the first of its kind

If architecture is a language, what does this building have to tell its surroundings? The concrete and steel cube is situated at a bend in the street like an oversized, carelessly discarded parcel. It takes several minutes to walk around it. Anyone doing so feels dwarfed – a sense that is not allayed by advancing along the central "school street" inside the building. Light shines in through skylights above the three staircases and also through a window front on the ground floor along the centrally aligned cafeteria at a slightly lower level.

It is truly impossible to overlook the school building in Berlin-Wedding's Schwyzer Strasse. It represents the meagre remains of the great West Berlin school-building campaign of the 1970s. Within only a few years, 15 new schools were erected: twelve of the thirteen secondary schools for seventh to tenth grades were constructed using identical methods, in addition to two comprehensive secondary schools that were also built in a similar way. The school in Schwyzer Strasse is the last of the twelve standard buildings to have survived. After years of asbestos removal, it has accommodated the Oberstufenzentrum Gesundheit I ("Vocational School, Health Care I") since 1997.

School building in Schwyzer Strasse, today's Oberstufenzentrum Gesundheit I (left), spider plant in a Berlin primary school

It is worth travelling back in time since Berlin is currently planning a new wave of school construction to cover the projected demand for 80,000 additional school places by the 2024/25 school year. The Senate intends to invest five and a half billion Euros in the development in the coming ten years – according to guidelines presented by an inter-disciplinary group of experts in 2017 to create more than 60 new schools. The state-owned housing association Howoge will build up to 30 of them.

The first two competitions for a total of ten to twenty primary schools were carried out during the summer of 2018. The call for tenders turned into a nasty surprise for many, because the European competition exclusively required modular school buildings. Fur-thermore, offices could only participate if they were also able to act as the general contractor. "That is a disadvantage for small, innovative offices", Christine Edmaier, President of the Berlin Chamber of Architects, explains. She wrote an open letter to the Mayor of Berlin and the involved Senators, which was also signed by several pro-fessional associations. Although most of the Berlin plots are not ideally proportioned, the signatories criticised the renewed requirement to use modular-type solutions, despite the negative experiences of the 1970s.

As in the current debate, there were two aspects at the time: great demand for new school places and new educational ideals. In 1968, West Berlin opened the first com-prehensive school (Gesamtschule) in the Federal Republic. In 1970, when forecasts calculated an increase of 20,000 pupils in grades seven to ten, the SPD-led Senate decided to establish new secondary schools as integrated comprehensive schools with

Ruin of the old Brøndby Secondary School in Lankwitz before its demolition in 2016

all the new secondary schools, there had already been considerable debate on whether it was more economical to convert them or demolish and rebuild them. In almost all cases, demolition was the preferred option.

It is not as if there had been no warnings about the risks. Building 13 schools in one stroke, 12 of which with identical types, was also considered risky at the time. For instance in late 1972, the architecture critic Günther Kühne bemoaned the lack of any feedback or correction process in an article in the daily *Der Tagesspiegel*. It was, "hard to imagine that a uniform concept based on a ground plan of 90 by 90 metres could be constructed without any negative impact in view of the plots' highly contrasting dimensions", Kühne wrote. At the time, seven of the schools were already being constructed.

However, there were insufficient funds and a lack of time for individual adaptation or too many scruples. Test buildings were not constructed due to political pressure, nor were experts consulted, for instance with respect to air conditioning, despite the architects' desire to do so. Instead, everything was standardised, including the costs: each school with a standard ground plan for 1,200 pupils respectively should cost 39 million D-Mark. "That went badly wrong", Christine Edmaier explains. "It shows what decision-making mistakes are possible."

all-day supervision from 8.00 to 16.00. The three tiers of the upper school system – high school (Gymnasium), secondary modern (Realschule) and lower secondary school (Hauptschule) – were to be abolished.

The goal of greater democracy for the education system was combined with a faith in progress, industry and technology. Before the competition, a group of experts from the fields of education and architecture, led by the Senator for Schools, defined the structural principles. Based on the role model of modern comprehensive schools such as those in the USA, it was decided to erect compact buildings with full air conditioning and artificial lighting in two fifths of the classrooms. Fixed classes were replaced by departmental rooms.

Serial construction was also an underlying condition of the architectural competition in 1971. 48 Berlin architectural teams participated, with eight qualifying for an optimisation stage in which they all had to develop a joint design: Ivan Krusnik and partners, Kurt Brohm and Wilhelm Kurth, Ruth Golan and Wolfgang Pohl, Sabine Klose and Klaus-Rüdiger Pankrath, Regina Poly and Karl-Heinz Steinebach.

Later, nobody was able to say exactly who had decided what, as Karl-Heinz Steinebach recalled in an interview in 1989 during an exhibition on the theme of asbestos at the Heimatmuseum Neukölln. At that time, after the discovery of asbestos in almost

Even while some of the schools were still being built, criticism began to pile up in the schools that had already opened: the air-conditioning often failed, there were complaints about lessons in windowless "dark rooms" and the flat roofs did not always keep out the rain. There was also damage due to vandalism. By late 1975, all the secondary schools had finally opened, but their reputation as exemplary projects had already been tarnished.

The final straw was the discovery of asbestos in all the secondary schools in the late 1980s. The pupils were transferred to provisional "school villages". Some of the school buildings were left to decay for years because there were no funds to demolish them. The situation also revealed the down side of the economic construction, as is incidentally the case in 2018: the client was the state-owned housing association Degewo, which rented the schools out to the districts for a period of 30 years. The rent still had to be paid even after the schools were no longer usable.

One error during the design process for the secondary schools was a failure to adapt exemplary projects from elsewhere to the local conditions. Not even their alignments were respected during the construction. Furthermore, although the schools were both public educational centres, with city library branches, adult education and youth clubs, the architecture made no reference to the surroundings.

It is an entirely different story with the institutions built during an earlier school-building campaign, many of which still exist today: Ludwig Hoffmann was Berlin's Director of Municipal Development (Stadtbaurat) between 1896 and 1924, a period of rapid expansion. Berlin had a million inhabitants for the first time in 1877. By 1900, the number had risen to 1.9 million. They all required an appropriate infrastructure. During his 28 years in office, Hoffmann designed numerous hospitals and public baths, as well as 69 schools. He too encountered a problem that again challenges school planners today: limited space. Most of the schools designed by Hoffmann were built in growing districts in eastern Berlin such as Prenzlauer Berg, Pankow and Friedrichshain, often on affordable peripheral plots with narrow street fronts. There were usually houses for teachers at the schools' front sides, with classrooms in the rear sections and side wings.

Hoffmann's schools were often also standardised, with a fixed spatial programme, as Dörte Döhl describes in her dissertation on the Stadtbaurat, which was published in 2004: the schools generally had 36 classrooms and one physics room, conference rooms, teaching-equipment rooms, crèches, one large assembly hall, a school canteen, a gym and a shower area. The classic school type has long corridors, classrooms of equal size and large window fronts. However, Hoffmann did design contrasting façades for each school: almost every one has a different design, often with decorative, ornamental details.

Ludwig Hoffmann's school buildings also reflect the educational trends of the time. It was a period when the education system was becoming increasingly diversified, so instead of building simple municipal schools, Hoffmann developed three distinct types of secondary school buildings as well as special vocational schools. Today's educational approaches view such classification more critically. However, the façades of Hoffmann's schools remain and are still harmoniously integrated into their surroundings today.

Heinrich-Schliemann-Gymnasium by Ludwig Hoffmann in Prenzlauer Berg

Montessori centre, Freising

Gute Änger 32
85356 Freising

GFA 6,375 m²
GV   25,975 m³

Numrich Albrecht Klumpp Gesellschaft von Architekten mbH
www.nak-architekten.de

Client: Montessori Landkreis Freising e. V.

Sports hall

Viewing window with seating frame

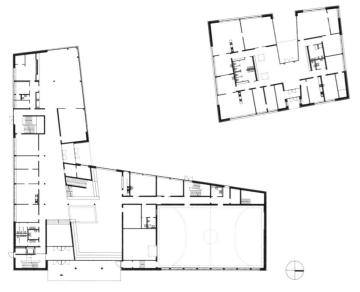

Ground floor plan

Atrium

New development of a school ensemble using a three-storey building for an all-day school with an integrated sports hall and a single-storey daycare centre. The day care centre accommodates a playgroup, crèche and kindergarten. Shielded from the street noise, the schoolyard is situated between the two buildings. For the new construction, the educational concept was applied to a spatial concept in close cooperation with the school management. Thus in the spirit of Montessori teaching, the functions are ordered in a clear and simple way. The foyer forms the core of the school and opens out towards the break area, café, canteen and other communal areas. An exercise area connects that central space to the more peaceful learning areas above them. The corridors are integrated into the teaching areas to provide sufficient space for flexible learning groups. The design concept combines all interior and exterior spaces to create a lively "school habitat".

View from the north (top), foyer (bottom)

All-day supervision, Leutenbach Comprehensive School

Theodor-Heuss-Strasse 27
71397 Leutenbach

GFA 1,075 m²
GV 4,425 m³

Wiechers Beck Gesellschaft von Architekten mbH
www.wiechers-beck.de

Client: Community of Leutenbach,
represented by the Mayor

View from the school building

Dining room by the canteen yard

New construction of a daycare centre with canteen for a comprehensive school.
The buildings are embedded into the topography of the schoolyard to preserve the
overall available space: their roof areas supplement the usable exterior area. The canteen
building forms the campus perimeter on its southwestern corner at street level. The
dining room with 200 seats opens towards the inner courtyard, from where outdoor
stairs lead to the upper level in front of the school building. A playground terrace is
situated there at street level, along with a copse of trees that borders with the building
for all-day supervision. That building (which is connected internally to the canteen
beneath it) initially only has one full floor with supervision rooms, one multifunctional
hall and offices. The upper level can be completed at a later date to create additional
supervision rooms. Until then, a framing element of perforated sheet metal envelops
the volume while the roof serves as a playing area and an open-air classroom.

Overall view from the west (top) floor plans, levels 1 and 2 (bottom)

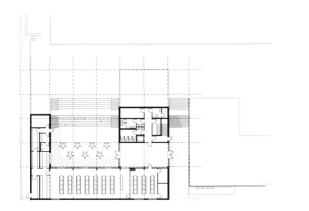

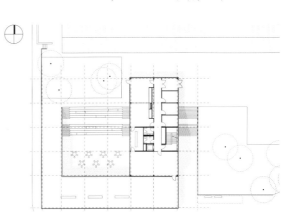

Primary school and daycare centre, Leipzig

Schreberstrasse 5–7
04109 Leipzig

GFA (new building)	2,525 m²
GFA (existing building)	1,500 m²
GV (new building)	10,525 m³
GV (existing building)	6,025 m³

W&V Architekten GmbH
www.wuv-architekten.de

Client: forum thomanum Schulen GmbH

Hall

Classroom

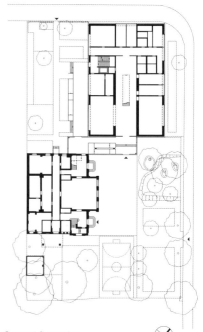

Ground floor plan

New construction of a school and conversion of a listed building into a daycare centre. The ensemble is the latest module of the forum thomanum, a music campus based around the St. Thomas Choir of Leipzig. The former parish hall of the Lutherkirche accommodates the day care centre rooms for this purpose. The *Gründerzeit* building had not been used for a long time and required an additional floor, while its original spatial structure was restored. A glass walkway connects the day care centre to the school. In the new building, flexibly usable classrooms surround three sides of the staircase. The ground floor is glazed, while the walls above consist of 70-centimetre thick, two-leaf brickwork – which is a plus for durability and energy efficiency. Long-distance heating energy covers heating requirements. A photovoltaic system on the school roof provides 40 percent of the power demands. The school building won the 2017 Architecture Prize of the City of Leipzig.

View from the street (top), ensemble from the east (bottom)

Zepernick Primary School extension

Schönerlinder Strasse 47 GFA 2,675 m²
16341 Panketal GV 10,225 m³

**ARGE Renner Architekten GmbH I
Bollinger+Fehlig Architekten GmbH**
www.rennerarchitekten.de

Client: Municipality of Panketal

Classroom with open playing corridor

Playing corridor

Group room

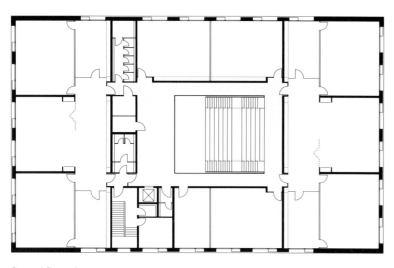

Ground floor plan

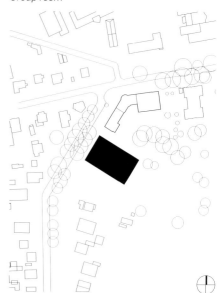

Plan

New development of a school building for three streams. An old building from the 1920s, a daycare centre and an extension outline the schoolyard on three sides. The new rooms complement the existing facility with concepts orientated towards contemporary education and new learning methods. At its centre, a flight of stairs leads up from a hall to a surrounding gallery level. This multifunctional forum is used for playing, as a gathering space and also for performances where the stairs are used as an auditorium. Teaching rooms form the building's head end with two clusters on each level. Each cluster consists of three classrooms, two group rooms and one playing corridor. The rooms can be individually combined thanks to the moveable interior walls. Outside, the solid structure presents a façade of bright bricks, concrete windowsills and broad windows. Their vents are situated behind panels of pearly-beige perforated metal sheeting.

View from the south (top), hall (bottom)

Arndt High School extension

Königin-Luise-Strasse 80
14195 Berlin

GFA 3,500 m²
GV 14,200 m³

AFF Architekten
www.aff-architekten.com

Client: District Authority of Steglitz-
Zehlendorf, Berlin

View from the east

Bridges to the old building

Communal area

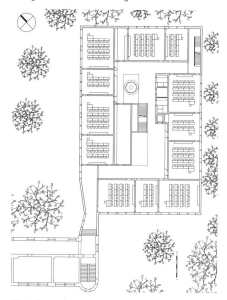
First floor plan

New construction of a school building following a competition in 2011. The three-storey building was erected at a respectful distance from the preservation-listed old building by the architects Friedrich and Wilhelm Hennings, which was constructed in 1909. Bridges on the first and second floors connect the buildings. The ground floor of the new building houses the library, canteen, staff studies and the school magazine's editorial department. The foyer forms the heart of the building with its large staircase in the atrium. The broad, open space can be used in diverse ways. Between classes, it also acts as a break area. The classrooms are arranged around the atrium on the first floor. Specially equipped science classrooms are organised in a similar fashion on the second floor.

School by the town hall

Rathausstrasse 8
10367 Berlin

GFA 3,900 m²
GV 16,000 m³

Numrich Albrecht Klumpp Gesellschaft von Architekten mbH
www.nak-architekten.de

Client: District Authority of Berlin-Lichtenberg, SE Facility Management

View from the south

Staircase

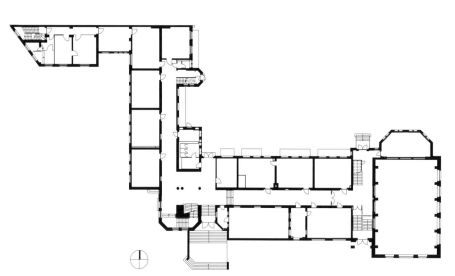

Ground floor plan

Baffle wall

Renovation of a school building built in 1910 in accordance with monument-preservation guidelines during running operations. The ensemble in a Neorenaissance style was conceived by the Berlin Director of Building Johannes Uhlig and the architect Wilhelm Grieme as a girls' secondary school with a headmaster's house. The project restored the façade with windows and exterior doors, as well as renovating the sports hall and assembly above it to conform to today's requirements. In the assembly hall, the 1950s walls, parquet flooring and box-type windows were enhanced and the original coffered ceiling was renovated. Six new pendant luminaires supplement the ceiling plate lights to achieve a contemporary lighting concept. The sports hall received a wooden baffle wall that also serves to store equipment. A ceiling radiant heater replaces the old heating system. The rooms' colour concept is based on restoration findings.

Sports hall (top), assembly hall (bottom)

Thünen Institute

Herwigstrasse 31　　GFA 14,300 m²　**Staab Architekten GmbH**　　Client: Federal Ministry of Food and Agriculture
27572 Bremerhaven　GV　67,200 m³　www.staab-architekten.com

Conference floor

Façade

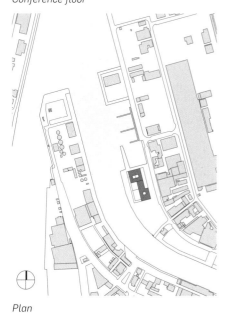

Plan

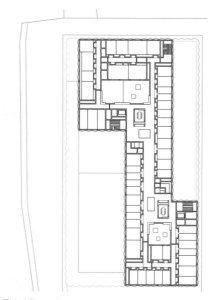

Third floor plan

New development for a federal research facility. The project is the result of a competition in 2012. The building in the rough environment of a fishing harbour accommodates the Thünen Institutes for Fisheries Ecology and Sea Fisheries. It provides a modern, high-performance infrastructure for research and improves communication between scientists. The colour effect of the folded aluminium façade reacts to the light in the harbour. Smoothly integrated folding shutters shield the laboratories from the sun. Above a base with storage and an aquaculture facility, the conference floor opens up towards the water with large terraces. The cubes of the two institutes develop above them. The laboratories and offices are arranged along the façades with a view of the water and the institutes' own research ships. Broad access areas connect the rooms and provide diverse opportunities for exchanging information.

View from the northwest (top), laboratory with closed façade (bottom)

Mirror, mirror on the wall

What architecture enthusiasts find attractive about Berlin

*Building site perimeter outside the Neue
Nationalgalerie by Ludwig Mies van der Rohe
(left), Holocaust Memorial by Peter Eisenman*

Berlin has always been a place of avant-garde architectural movements. But what is the state of building culture in the city today? What draws people from outside to it? Which qualities inspire people to travel there?

José Ezquiaga Domínguez is an architect and Director of the Madrid Chamber of Architects (COAM). One of the reasons why the Spaniard is so attracted to Berlin is the variety of its styles from the past and present. "Some of my professional colleagues claim you can't understand Madrid without grasping Berlin", Domínguez comments. He claims it is "the result of centuries of exchange between Spanish and German designing architects". In his opinion, the ability to reinvent oneself out of almost nothing distinguishes Berlin to this day. Berlin is indeed a city of repeated upheaval: industrial revolution, Hobrecht, the 1920s and the reform movement, war and Germania, division, reunification and the current boom – all of which and more can be read in the city.

If one asks designing architects and enthusiasts from abroad which buildings they recommend to travellers with little time, the usual suspects top the list: Peter Eisenman's Holocaust Memorial, Foster's Reichstag dome, Libeskind's Jewish Museum, the New Museum redeveloped by David Chipperfield and even a structure that is no longer there: the Wall. The Kulturforum is occasionally mentioned due to its classic Modern buildings: Mies van der Rohe's Nationalgalerie, Hans Scharoun's Philharmonie and the Staatsbibliothek.

However, Hulya Ertas, Editor in Chief of the Turkish architectural magazine *XXI*, recommends going beyond individual buildings: "I find the urban structures even more attractive. Each time I walk through its streets, Berlin gives me this strange sense of familiarity. That is remarkable in a city that I visit for only a few days." The journalist speculates whether the familiarity stems from the fact that Berlin, "like all global cities of today, has no specific identity. Berlin is one of those matured cities where you can spend your time in a relaxed way. By comparison, Istanbul seems like a teenager since everyone is so keen to enjoy the city."

Thus not only the free-standing buildings, but equally their integration into the overall structure are what characterises Berlin, as Sönke Schneidewind, the Cultural Manager of the urban marketing company visitBerlin, explains: "Berlin is a city of neighbourhood developments." In addition to the *Gründerzeit* quarters of the 19th century and the traces of industrial culture and "Elektropolis", reform housing development, including 1920s estates and post-war Modern construction, also provides exciting reasons to explore the city. Especially on the 100th anniversary of the Bauhaus movement, the urban advertising expert encourages visitors to turn their attention to Bauhaus and

Residential building by Hans Scharoun in the extensive Siemensstadt housing estate (1929–1931)

post-war architecture: the Haselhorst estate, the Ernst Reuter estate, the Hansa quarter, the structures along Karl-Marx-Allee, the Schaubühne and Woga-complex ensemble, and especially the six developments of Berlin's Modernity that UNESCO has given the status of World Heritage, all of which reflect exciting, historically determined functional interconnections.

But what about more recent developments? After the end of Germany's division, the city rapidly restored its status as a metropolis in the mid-1990s. That was exactly the time when Dominique Perrault came to Berlin. The Frenchman designed the velodrome and adjoining swimming facility for Berlin's bid to host the 2000 Olympics. "I sensed the enthusiasm following the fall of the Wall, when Berlin was one big building site and no longer isolated." In the last 20 years, he believes the city has developed faster than any other in Europe. "It is no longer the same city, with brownfields and dilapidated ruins at every corner." The city has experienced an enormous transformation. "Before the fall of the Wall, there were the utopias of Modernity, a symbolic relationship to history, which greatly affected urban planning." By contrast, the utopias of the 1990s have remained unfulfilled wishes, as hardly any of them were actually constructed. "For instance the future of the Tempelhofer Feld is symptomatic. People do gardening on it, play sports and use it locally. But the territorial dimension is completely underestimated." The 350-hectare Tempelhof grounds, which are larger than New York's Central Park, should instead be regarded as part of a "greater Berlin... in a global dimension". Perrault recommends that tourists visiting the city for only a short time should definitely see the former airport, a view shared by Finn Geipel. The architect is equally at home in Paris and Berlin, but has a more qualified opinion concerning brownfields: "Paradoxically, brownfields make the lack of anything to experience tangible, thereby reminding us of transience. In that sense, they cannot be 'used' at all."

Thibaut de Ruyter, a French architect who has lived and worked as a curator and critic in Berlin since 2001 believes that serious errors were made by planners, the building sector and politicians in the 1990s: "The empty properties were simply filled without recognising their true potential, all with the aim of eradicating the traces of history and reconstructing an idealised pre-1933 Berlin! You only have to look at what is happening to the Berlin Palace and the area around it." Back then, Berlin stopped experimenting: "There was an international building fair in 1957 and then another in 1987. What did we get in 2017? Nothing." Asked for a label to describe his chosen city of residence, de Ruyter names a tune by the jazz pianist Thelonious Monk: Ugly Beauty.

The association is not without parallel. After the turn of the millennium, the city lent its name to the coarsely charming *Berlin Style*. It represented more an outlook on life than a true architectural style, but has had a definitive effect on the image of Berlin in other countries in recent decades. The attitude is characterised by industrial rawness, the charm of improvisation and the art of translating defects into hip coolness, climaxing in the motto "Poor, but sexy". Today's new collective movements are closely connected to that spirit and it is in them that Hulya Ertas sees a continuation of the old joy of experimentation. José Ezquiaga Domínguez also believes that Berlin has by no means run out of steam renewing itself: "Time and time again, it appears in thousands of ways and forms." The drawing boards of political and urban planning in major cities like Madrid and Berlin have been reconfigured by the rise of social movements and citizens' initiatives. Today, Berlin is a city that is reinventing and recycling itself: "I would even go as far as saying that the task of conceiving a flexible, energetically sustainable city and creating new hybrid spaces for new ways of life in the city represents a scenario in which Berlin's experiences are an inspiration to everyone throughout Europe."

In Berlin, the current boom and resulting housing shortage are regarded more as hindrances on the path to quality and innovation. The view is different abroad. With respect to the lack of housing, Domínguez believes debate should focus on what type of housing, rather than how many apartments should be built. Building large volumes quickly requires a variety of formats that can cope with the diversity of situations in Berlin. Finn Geipel believes that not only applies to building typologies, but also to new forms of development and new kinds of developers.

Hulya Ertas stresses: "We can already see interesting approaches in joint building ventures and co-housing experiments in Berlin. And there is always space for innovation if you take the time for it and refrain from setting solutions in concrete all too quickly. Questions concerning affordability and mass production can even be rewarding if they are taken into account with the right sensitivity during the design and development process for new buildings." Ultimately, urban density is essential for an economically, ecologically and socially strong city. Nevertheless, Ertas does not believe the population issue can be solved within the city limits alone. "To ensure a city remains liveable, it may be necessary to limit its population density. That also means developing cities in an equally powerful and desirable way elsewhere in the country."

The exciting question of how Berlin will cope with the challenges of the latest growth spurt is another reason to follow the recommendation made by Sönke Schneidewind: anyone visiting Berlin should return at least every three to five years and see what has changed. "Berlin visitors could then enjoy the summer nights on the perron outside Chipperfield's James Simon Gallery", Schneidewind comments. Or you can go and explore a less famous little gem, such as Finn Geipel's tip: a trip to Caputh to see Einstein's house designed by Konrad Wachsmann.

Einstein's house in Caputh, designed by Konrad Wachsmann

Futurium Berlin

Alexanderufer 2
10117 Berlin

GFA 14,000 m²
GV 89,300 m³

RICHTER MUSIKOWSKI
www.richtermusikowski.com

Client: Institute for Federal Real Estate

Northern gallery exhibition space, upper floor

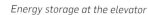

Energy storage at the elevator

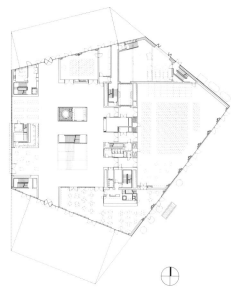

Ground floor plan

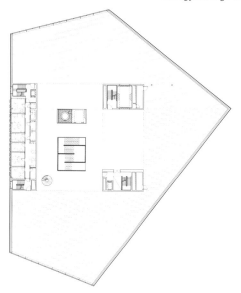

Upper floor plan

New development of an exhibition and event building. The project is the result of an open competition in 2011. The Futurium's aim is to make forward-looking developments visible and encourage dialogue between research and development. Situated between the Federal Ministry of Research, the Charité, Humboldthafen and the Central Station, the folded-open building presents an autonomous sculptural form. Forecourts towards the River Spree and the S-Bahn mark its main entrances. On the roof, a public skywalk leads around and through the solar panels. Inside, the building is structured into three areas: the Futurium Lab in the basement is a workshop and pioneering laboratory; the Forum on the ground floor is a meeting place and event platform. Permanent exhibitions and administration are accommodated on the upper level. The building was awarded Gold Certification by the Federal Assessment System for Sustainable Building.

View from the Charité

View from the south (top), foyer (bottom)

Spreehalle Berlin

Reinbeckstrasse 20
12459 Berlin

GFA 2,975 m²
GV 13,025 m³

**HOIDN WANG PARTNER, Feilden Clegg
Bradley Studios, with Sauerzapfe Architekten**
www.hoidnwang.de

Client: Bryan Adams

Exterior view from the southwest

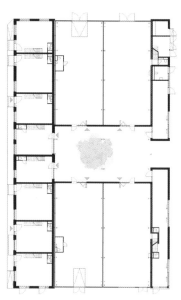

Ground floor plan

Studio in the hall

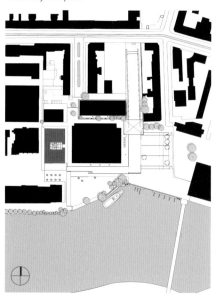

Plan

Conversion of a two-winged production hall with side sections in the old industrial quarter of Oberschöneweide by the River Spree. The ensemble houses studios, a café, a bookshop and other commercial activities. A new courtyard at the centre of the hall serves as a communal retreat area. Above it, the roof cladding was removed, while the steel load-bearing structure was retained. The rest of the hall is divided into four studios, with eight more in the side sections. A massive two-storey structure, which was originally used for administration, was heightened with a six-metre studio floor for this purpose. The distribution of the eight studio buildings was derived from the situation of the windows in the existing structure. A north-light and windows on two sides provide those studios with natural light. Steel sliding windows lead from the steel galleries to a balcony with a view of the Spree. The old single-storey changing room wing along the other hall flank is replaced by a new two-storey development on the same space.

Studio in the side section

Artist's studio and house

| Ohmstrasse 12 | GFA 670 m² | **Philipp von Matt Architect BDA** | Client: Bernard Frize |
| 10179 Berlin | GV 3,775 m³ | phvm.com | |

View from the street

Living room

Plan

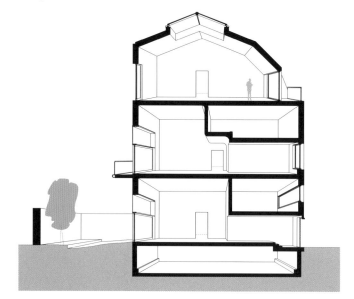
Section

New building for living and creative working. The property in a narrow side street was once part of a row of *Gründerzeit* houses with a height of only 11.5 metres. The Mitte heating plant is situated directly opposite. The surroundings of old housing and single-storey factories are now dominated by the club scene and nightlife. Broad war-induced brownfields are scattered around the building. The new building's client is a painter who required a showroom on the ground floor with an inserted gallery floor for guests. The showroom is directly connected to the garden. The levels above house the apartment and a studio beneath the roof including a rooftop loggia. The interior design concept was to already achieve the finished condition of the rooms during the shell construction stage, so far as this was possible. That approach especially characterises the concrete staircase.

Staircase and studio (top), showroom (bottom)

Garage

Baumschulenstrasse 1b
12437 Berlin

GFA 105 m²
GV 440 m³

Tanja Lincke Architekten GmbH
www.tanja-lincke-architekten.com

Client: private

Garage segment

Conversion of a triple garage building by the River Spree. A new thermal interior
envelope and the insertion of building technology for amenities paved the way to use
the 1970s structure in a flexible way. When the doors are closed, the transformation is
invisible. Outside, only the rough plaster was painted in black, like the adjacent depot
building. The old appearance of the garage doors remains unchanged. The even trisection
of the new glass façade behind them follows the rhythm of the doors, but the horizontal bars allow it to remain an autonomous element. A supply area with access from all
three units has been inserted at the rear of the central segment.

View from the northeast (top), floor plan, access to the supply area (bottom)

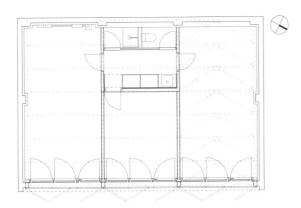

Peering round the corner

Schifferberg 2a 18347 Ahrenshoop	GFA (new building) GFA (existing building) GV (new building) GV (existing building)	30 m² 225 m² 105 m³ 600 m³	**gorinistreck architekten** www.gorinistreckarchitekten.de	Client: Charlotte Streck

Landscape window

New construction of an artist's studio. The small studio and gallery building is situated on the stretch of land between the Baltic Sea and the peninsula bay. The client aims to use it for art that encourages a dialogue with the natural and cultural region of the Baltic Sea. The new building supplements a house from the 1940s and extends from its rear section, looking around the corner into the landscape. The stilted building is inserted into the dense tree population of the dune landscape. Like the minimal footprint of its foundation in the landscape, the ecological footprint was reduced as far as possible: the building is a pure timber construction including its finishing and insulation materials. Only the exterior is clad in clay shingles in a reference to the brickwork of the house. In the bright interior, a window that covers an entire wall frames the view of the landscape.

Model

Studio space (top), plan, clay shingles (bottom)

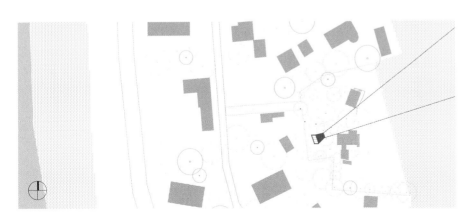

More space to share
Without cars, the entire city becomes an open space

Parks and squares in the city are places to pause and take a deep breath. They offer protection from noise, hectic urban activity and above all the traffic. That is how open spaces have been planned for decades: detached and sheltered, while cars have priority. Criticism of that situation is not new. But it was not until the Deutsche Umwelthilfe took the car industry to court for fraudulent nitrogen oxide levels that it seemed possible to reduce the volume of traffic to a humanly compatible scale. The "free" aspect of open spaces has thereby gained an entirely new significance. Instead of simply keeping them clear, it also expressed true liberty: the freedom to shape outdoor spaces in the entire city. The path to a transport turnaround is still rather rocky, but debate on the subject has become much more serious and one can already see good examples in many cities.

One spectacular example is the liberation of the River Sieg from the so-called Siegplatte. Now hardly conceivable, the City of Siegen placed a concrete plate over the River Sieg for parking spaces in the late 1960s. When the structure began to crumble, it was seen as an opportunity to tear it down. Today, silver willow trees and tall, broad steps line the riverbank. People meet for a chat where once only cars were parked. Planners of urban and open spaces call it "quality of stay".

So onwards to new shores! Or to the "revitalisation of locations", as the transport expert Thomas Stein from the Deutsches Institut für Urbanistik (German Institute of Urban Affairs) explains: "If streets and squares are not attractive and usable, they're no use to people." It is not easy to plan streets and squares well, as can be seen in the first two "encounter zones" the Berlin Senate has established as part of its pedestrian strategy.

For instance people have mainly rejected the Maassenstrasse encounter zone between Nollendorfplatz and Winterfeldtplatz due to its poor aesthetic quality. Naively painted concrete bollards partition the pedestrian area from the street; the metal benches positioned there have no backrests and the overall design looks dreary. And yet good design, good details and good materials are the quality criteria of a city on a human scale. At least that is what the Danish architect and urban planner Jan Gehl believes. He was responsible for partially pedestrianising Times Square in New York. However, a before-and-after study of Maassenstrasse by the office LK Argus has positive aspects to report as well: "The number of pedestrians has increased by around 30 percent. Waiting times to cross the road have fallen." One important goal of the car-restricting urban planning has therefore been achieved: "The aim is to break down the separating effect of streets and bring their left and right sides together", Stein explains. Yet the other encounter zone in Berlin's pilot project suggests the Senate still needs some

Parklet in Bergmannstrasse, Berlin-Kreuzberg (left), steps along the River Sieg in Siegen

Maassenstrasse "encounter zone" in Berlin-Schöneberg

practice. Benches in a U-shaped alignment, which have the pretty name of "parklets", have been installed in Bergmannstrasse since the spring of 2018. Invented in San Francisco, parklets are seating arrangements on parking spaces. In Bergmannstrasse, they are mainly arranged with their backs to the street so that people gathering there have the noise of the traffic behind them. That is unacceptable from a psychological perspective. It also neglects another of Gehl's principles, namely "beautiful views". Enjoying the Bergmannstrasse townscape with its Wilhelminian façades is not part of the plan, since the parklets are aligned in a way that forces people to look at the ground floor of the adjacent building. It is almost intrusive.

However, the idea of reclaiming the street from cars, or in this case parking spaces, is certainly a good thing. 90 percent of urban space in the city is occupied by cars that are either travelling or parking (mostly for free). That space is unavailable for other uses. According to street legislation, the primary object of streets is to serve traffic. Moving or parked cars are what is known as "common utilisation". Everything else is special utilisation. In concrete terms, that means every bar or restaurant that places

a few chairs in front of its door requires a permit. Cars do not. It seems that even well-meaning planners find it very hard to shrug off the perceived right that cars have with respect to the street space. The German Road Safety Council (DVR) believes planners are often too heavily involved in daily business, so they at best recognise and view well-designed streets by chance. In the publication *Gute Straßen in Stadt und Dorf* (Good streets in cities and villages), the TH Köln – University of Applied Sciences has therefore presented examples to the Road Safety Council that fulfil a further demand in Gehl's vision: they satisfy a desire for safety that is especially experienced by pedestrians and cyclists.

Bahnhofstrasse in Cottbus has achieved minor fame in this respect: multiple use is one of the key ideas of a more liveable city, as can be seen in Cottbus. A central lane, over three metres wide, has been transformed into an island at particularly frequented places for pedestrians to cross the road. At junctions, it changes its function and transforms into a left-turning lane for cars. The space-saving lane guidance even enables an avenue of trees, while the street cross-section now has the same dimensions as it had before the conquest of the automobile.

Thomas Stein's vision of a successful campaign to reclaim public space is as follows: "You don't have to watch out at every junction whether a 20-tonne truck is charging past. The city is not car-free, but automobiles are reduced to a more tolerable level. And people can meet and communicate throughout the city, rather than just at allocated places." Thus inversely, planning in the car-restricted age should not only affect attractive medieval market squares to remove their through-traffic. For instance in Berlin, the impressive GDR thoroughfares and their flanking open spaces should also be considered and made more liveable.

A prefabricated housing estate in Potsdam-Drewitz is exemplary in this respect. The key measure of overhauling the quarter was to convert Konrad-Wolf-Allee, an unnecessarily broad throughroad, into a district park. "Despite the considerable noise due to the traffic and a high level of sealed surfaces, the residents were initially concerned about the loss of parking spaces", as the Federal Environment Agency explains in its readable brochure entitled *Straßen und Plätze neu denken* (Rethinking streets and squares). Ten percent of the parking spaces were indeed sacrificed for the conversion measures. However, parking management continued to guarantee a parking space for everyone who lives there. It is surprising how much space was created by reducing the number of parking spaces and the width of the road lanes. The gained space was used for new paths, playgrounds, gathering spaces with fountains, seating and climbing rocks. In 2014, the concept won the Deutsche Städtebaupreis (German Urban Development Award).

Temporary measures have a great deal of charm when it comes to demonstrating alternative uses of public space. "Once people have experienced the quality and the open spaces a street without cars can offer, they are often motivated to support its permanent conversion", Stein explains. Those voices are important when parking spaces are being discussed, if not before.

Ultimately, like all planning, the key is well-conceived details. For instance in Cologne, they managed to kill two birds with one stone by setting up bicycle stands that also act as obstacles to prevent illegal parking there. A disorganised mess of parked bikes also undermines the quality of stay in an urban location, even though bicycles are preferable to cars. By contrast, there is still an urgent need for a solution to delivery vehicles, a sector that continues to grow in times of online trade. In the project City2Share, the Deutsches Institut für Urbanistik is investigating how private and delivery transport in Munich's city centre can be combined into an overall concept. The plan envisages mobility stations – including cycle hire, car sharing and a hub for local public transport. In this way, urban and transport planning both play an increasingly significant role for the open spaces of the future. The approach remains the same for all disciplines: if there are fewer cars, there is more space to share.

District park along Konrad-Wolf-Allee in Potsdam-Drewitz

Hublandpark Würzburg

| Rottendorfer Strasse 97074 Würzburg | Area 230,000 m² | **hutterreimann Landschaftsarchitektur GmbH** www.hr-c.net | Client: Landesgartenschau Würzburg 2018 GmbH |

Garden terrace

Wiesenpark fountain

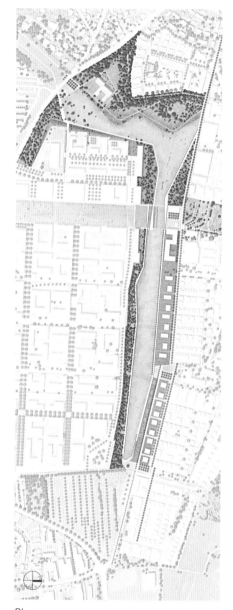
Plan

Newly designed urban park. The project is the result of a competition in 2012. Hubland is a new district on the terrain of an abandoned US military base, where apartments for several thousand people and a university and research campus have been under development since 2009. The central open space – once a runway for the military airport – was designed as a broad park for the 2018 State Garden Show. The terrain is situated at a relatively high altitude, thereby providing a view of the city's silhouette and the Marienberg fortress. The park's underlying structure is the Beltwalk – a tour of its perimeter. An urban landscape park with terrace gardens and playgrounds was created while taking the old tree population and impressive natural stone walls into account. Large "urban squares" serve as entrance connections to the surrounding residential and research quarters.

→ Project 38 on pages 98/99 for the Belvedere platform

Garden terraces (top), square by the climbing plane (bottom)

Volmepark Kierspe

| Volmestrasse 149 | Area | **Franz Reschke Landschaftsarchitektur** | Client: City of Kierspe |
| 58566 Kierspe | 30,000 m² | www.franzreschke.de | |

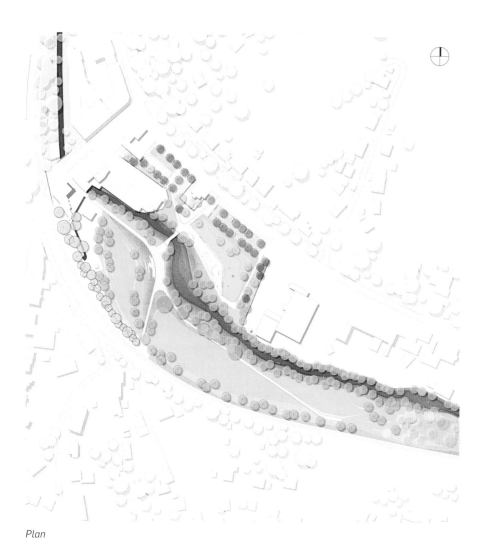

Plan

Playing sculpture

Park entrance marking

New design of a park following a competition in 2014. The park in the district of Kierspe-Bahnhof was established at the same time as the River Volme was renaturalised. Both measures were part of the Regionale 2013, a structural enhancement programme by the state for the region of South Westphalia. The open space stretches along the small river, on the one side extensively nature-orientated and on the other designed in an intensively urban way. To the south of the Volme, the park is largely near-natural. The "Weitblick" (a high viewing point) and a platform are situated there. Seating steps on the meadow slope serve as terraces. A new bridge by Jan Derveaux and Rimpau & Bauer Architekten connects the landscape side to the opposite bank. Active spaces consisting of concrete topographies and playing installations line the riverbank. Steel elements refer to the location's metal processing history.

Active area (top), view towards the bridge and stage square (bottom)

Nordhafenpark Berlin

| 10557 Berlin | Area
31,000 m² | **relais Landschaftsarchitekten Heck Mommsen PartGmbB**
www.relaisla.de | Client: State of Berlin and Bayer Pharma AG |

Northeastern bank

Relaxation area by the water

Plan

Design of a neighbourhood park following a competition in 2011. As the Europacity develops, the new role of the open spaces around the Nordhafen basin is becoming increasingly important. Until now, post-war park structures dominated the banks beneath the Nordhafenbrücke. The new design connects the western section and its eastern counterpart, which was funded by Bayer Pharma. Landscape steps and seating edges along the paths guide the view to the water. The fluent network of walkways follows the relief of the terrain. The side paths meander like old branches of a river and have a decelerating effect. References to the past have remained visible: old crane locations, the historical outlet structure and a ferry mooring have all received uniform railings and ground surfaces made of bulb plate in a reference to the basin's technical past. The architectural garden spaces, walls and steps in the 1950s park design were restored.

View from the western bank (top), landscape steps (bottom)

Community park, playing and sports area on the Grüner Bogen, Paunsdorf

04329 Leipzig | Area 11,200 m² | **häfner jiménez betcke jarosch landschaftsarchitektur gmbh** www.haefner-jimenez.de | Client: City of Leipzig

Community park from the south

Section on the southern bank

Playing and sports area

Barrier-free fishing area

New design of two recreation areas. Following a competition in 2000, the Grüner Bogen park area around the major Paunsdorf-Nord estate has been under development in the north of Leipzig for a number of years. To the west of the estate, a community park has been created for the 17,000 people living there. The landscaped lake is also used for fishing and a near-natural rainwater retention system for the neighbouring Heiterblick industrial estate. The earth excavated to create the lake was modelled into two hills. A viewing platform with barrier-free access is situated on one of them. At the foot of the hill, there is a meeting place for young people including playing facilities. The second area is situated at the southwestern tip of the arch, on the reinforced concrete foundations of a former supermarket centre. Parts of the foundations were broken up to insert cobblestone-framed hills with tree populations. Sports and playing areas are situated on the surrounding newly-asphalted surfaces.

Top of the northern hill in the community park (top), playing and sports area (bottom)

Windeck, Sieg waterfall

| Schönecker Weg 5 | Area | **bbzl böhm benfer zahiri** | Client: Community of Windeck |
| 51570 Windeck-Schladern | 7,000 m² | www.bbzl.de | |

Plan

Seating by the cultural centre

Outline of the former river route

Profiling of a river and industrial landscape following a competition in 2008. The path of the River Sieg characterises the landscape around the district of Schladern. During the period of industrialisation, the river was heavily realigned to ease freight transport and generate power. In parts, the interaction between human measures and nature has developed diverse spaces with impressive views. However, there was no clear transition between important public spaces and the surrounding natural areas. Three interventions have changed that: a cycle and foot path with viewing balconies runs along the railway ridge. It has thereby become a central axis in the texture of public spaces. Secondly, a series of special locations have been highlighted with respect to their relationship to the landscape. The third intervention was the expansion of the cycle and foot path network. Junction squares now accentuate important branches to those paths.

Steps by the crane railway (top), path along the railway ridge, Sieg waterfall (bottom)

Departure into the landscape

Oud Stationsplein
Helkijnstraat 79
8554 Zwevegem-Sint Denijs
(Belgium)

Area
2,650 m²

100Landschaftsarchitektur
www.100land.de

Client: Province of West Flanders and
the Community of Zwevegem

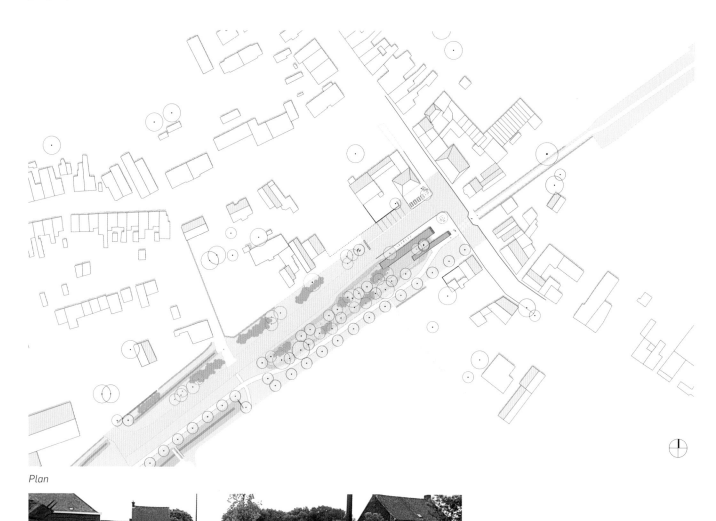

Plan

View from the southwest

Redesign of the station square. The station Sint Denijs was part of the Belgian regional railway network that was almost completely dismantled between the 1960s and 1980s. The station square at the village periphery had therefore become a neglected location. Today, the square has been revitalised by the new design. The historical cobble-stones now stretch over the perpendicular through road. The pavement in front of a café was widened into a patio. The most conspicuous innovation is a narrative aspect: two platforms made of locally typical red brick refer to the cultural-historical context by quoting both the railway platform and the station building. The abstract elements are a combined platform, seating arrangement, spatial partition and milestone: they connect the village square to the new cycle and foot paths in the surrounding field landscape.

Platforms

ArchTriumph Pavilion 2018

Museum Gardens
E29PA London
(Great Britain)

Area
70 m²

Julie Biron Architektin
www.juliebiron.eu

Client: ArchTriumph

3-D tile image

Temporary installation in the garden of the Victoria & Albert Museum of Childhood during the London Festival of Architecture. The pavilion design is tendered internationally every year. The only design and spatially-formative element of the winning entry in 2018 was the material of the tile. Individual classic tiles were threaded together on steel ropes to form a net. The result was a transparent curtain. Several intermeshed shells, each with a tile pattern, framed a relaxation area at the centre of the structure. The patterns overlapped both from the outside and inside to create complex three-dimensional compositions. These layered images changed constantly depending on the viewer's perspective.

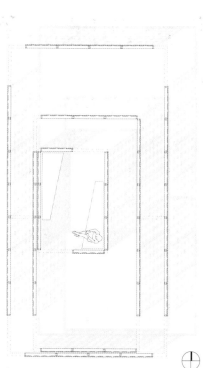

Ground plan

Overall view (top) and detail (bottom)

Bunkerberg elevated walkways

Collegienstrasse 53
06886 Lutherstadt
Wittenberg

Area
710 m²

**Architekturwerkstatt Berlin | imagine structure |
Düsseldorf University of Applied Sciences,
Department of Spatial and Sculptural Design**
www.aw-berlin.de

Client: Reformationsjubiläum 2017 e. V.

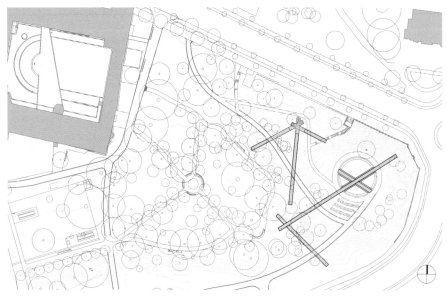

Plan

Elevated walkways

View towards the heaven's roof

Walkable installation following an art competition for the Reformation 2017 World
Fair. The ensemble of six elevated walkways was built on a hill covering a bunker ruin
from World War II. It rises up at the eastern end of the Luthergarten, which forms part
of the UNESCO World Heritage site. The walkway balustrades are mirrored, reflecting
nature, the garden and people. They also create new visual relationships and connections within Wittenberg. Due to the topography of the terrain, the walkways are stilted
in some places using supports up to eight metres long. They project into the landscape
at the edges of the garden. At one level junction, a "heaven's roof" reflects the earth
and sky depending on the viewing perspective. Diagonal surfaces reflecting the visitors
accompany the other junction on the top of the hill.

Stilts and heaven's roof

Albrecht Hausdorfer Secondary School playground

Kurzebracker Weg 40
13503 Berlin

Area
3,200 m²

**HAHN HERTLING VON HANTELMANN
Landschaftsarchitekten GmbH BDLA**
www.hhvh-landschaftsarchitekten.de

Client: District Authority of Reinickendorf, Berlin

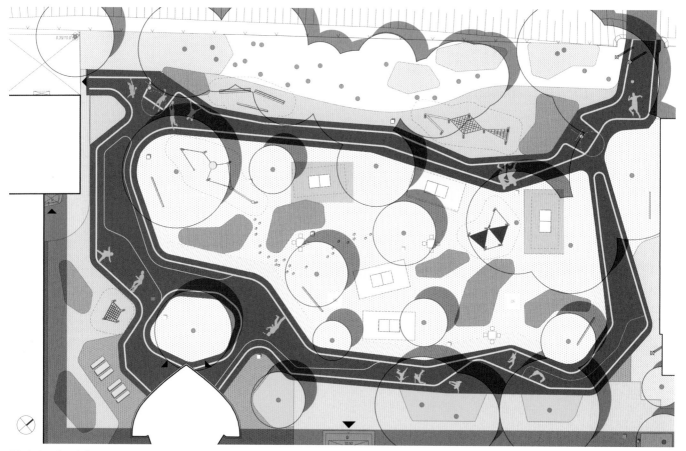

Workshop (top left), plan (bottom)

Redesigned school playground. The new construction of a canteen on part of the schoolyard, which already needed renovation, provided the occasion for the new design. During the maintenance work, a vehicle path was integrated into the terrain – for daily deliveries to the canteen and for fire services. The organic form of the asphalt tour of the yard is integrated into and between the dense tree population. Graphic symbols on the asphalt animate children to exercise: they are not only lines that mark the route of the path, but also depictions of young people in movement. These "dancing silhouettes" are based on a workshop with pupils, presenting a wide range of movements. Thus the children have participated in designing their own playground and are therefore closely tied to it. Bright yellow beams and rope elements on which to sit and balance also pick up on the theme of movement.

Asphalt graphics (top row), northeastern bend of the tour (bottom)

Viertel Zwei Plus

Stella-Klein-Löw-Weg
1020 Vienna
(Austria)

Area
21,425 m²

WES LandschaftsArchitektur PartG mbB
Schatz, Betz, Kaschke, Wehberg-Krafft,
Rödding with H. H. Krafft
www.wes-la.de

Client: IC Development GmbH

Plan

Northern courtyard

Exterior grounds for a new residential neighbourhood with offices. The urban quarter called Viertel Zwei is situated in the west of Vienna between the trade fair grounds, the new campus of the Economics University, the Krieau trotting racetrack and the Ernst Happel Stadium. The car-free area provides space for more than 4,500 people to live and work. The Viertel Zwei Plus extends the neighbourhood towards the Prater. Like the Viertel Zwei beside it, green islands characterise the open space at its northern end. An open square with a temporary water area forms the centre of the new facility. The water surface merges with the square and is subtly visible on the ground. Towards the south, at the transition to the Volkspark Prater, the open spaces condense into a landscape of broadly rolling grass hills among loose treetops. The walkways in between recall winding forest paths.

Square with water area (top), southern network of walkways (bottom)

Cloud garden in Brandenburg

Seestrasse 14467 Potsdam	Area 810 m²	**capattistaubach GbR** www.capattistaubach.de	Client: private

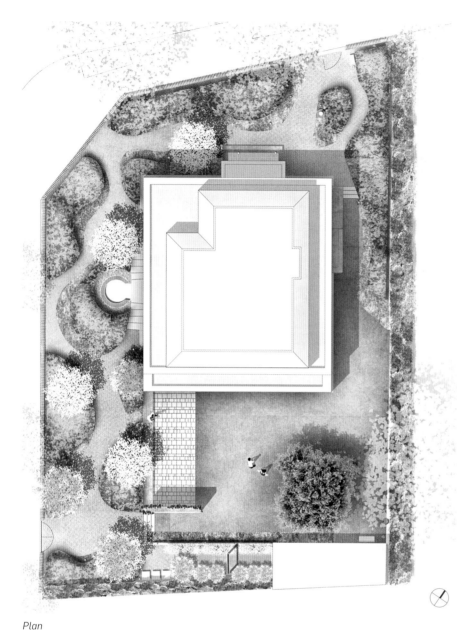

Plan

Flowering shrubs

Climbing roses

Redesigned private garden. The front garden along two sides of a corner property is characterised by a line of cloud-shaped privet bushes that remain green in the winter, with scattered apple and pear trees. The minimal measures provide maximum diversity for this part of the garden. Visually and in terms of the spatial experience, the constant alternation between spaces and shrubs creates the sense of a labyrinth. Planted shrubs accompany the topiary and create colourful and blooming accentuation that changes depending on the season. In the spring, they are complemented by lush scattered spring-flowering plants. The slightly lower area behind the house remains clear for use as a gathering area framed by a wall, a pergola with tall trellises and an auxiliary building. The solitary pine on the lawn is an eye-catcher.

Privet cloud in the front garden (top), detail, lawn behind the house (bottom)

Is that still Berlin?

New quarters and subculture biotopes

RAW estate in Berlin-Friedrichshain (left), Ostbahnhof quarter building site

The phenomenon is most conspicuous on Warschauer Brücke, as Kreuzbergers, Friedrichshainers and holidaymakers stand still for a moment, briefly glancing at the East Side Mall, the Mercedes-Benz Arena, all the new entertainment facilities around them, the Daimler offices and the Zalando headquarters. Only Berlin's municipal refuse company, the BSR, is still operating as it has always done. The fascinated observers turn their backs on the development work, shaking their heads in consternation and continue on their way. Anyone strolling in either direction on the bridge between Friedrichshain and Kreuzberg need not enter the new quarter by Ostbahnhof, a district that appears to be the spawn of a catalogue of investment architecture. But it is no longer possible to ignore it.

Nor can the developments be overlooked by the Baukollegium Berlin, the board that advises the Senate Building Director Regula Lüscher. It has the unenviable task of making the new Berlin and its façades compatible with the older structures: greater quality in terms of architecture and urban planning, more audacity in finding individual solutions, and less production-line development. So the Kollegium addressed the 140-metre high East Side Tower that is intended as the crowning piece of the Ostbahnhof quarter. After the Kollegium's meeting, Regula Lüscher stated that the 36-storey high-rise building designed by the Copenhagen Bjarke Ingels Group is still too smooth: "This is not Shanghai, not Singapore. This is Berlin." Instead, the tower should be rather "raw and wild". But is that even possible? A façade that reflects its environment? Bridging the gap between old and new?

Daniel Wesener would say it depends. The former leader of the Berlin Green Party has been following the development work at Warschauer Brücke for a long time at meetings of the Friedrichshain-Kreuzberg District Council. He has observed the lengthy delay with which new development projects are gradually noticed by the general public. "Not many people are interested when the development plans are being discussed", Wesener explains. "But years later, when building work starts on projects that have already been determined, there is great surprise."

So now, Kreuzbergers and Friedrichshainers stand on the bridge and ask themselves: Why didn't we prevent that? Wesener is sure that even with a "raw and wild" tower, the new quarter will not be integrated into the district's everyday life. It will remain an implant, an alien entity. So it is almost a blessing that the new investors' world is shielded from the old Berlin on three sides: to the south by the River Spree, to the north by the railway line and to the east by Warschauer Brücke.

The situation is entirely different to the east of Warschauer Brücke. Instead of an investor's dream, a different world has come to life there, namely the dream of the alternative, disordered, wild city. The RAW estate on Revaler Strasse is included in every Berlin

Warschauer Brücke between Kreuzberg and Friedrichshain

city guide. Locations such as the Astra Kulturhaus are must-see venues for partying visitors to the city. But there too, things will change, as new and old aspects meet. In 2015, the entrepreneur Lauritz Kurth purchased a large proportion of the estate for € 25 million. Since Kurth does not want to speculate with the estate, it must earn money to achieve a return on investment.

Florian Schmidt agrees. The former musician and graduate urban sociologist has been the Friedrichshain-Kreuzberg Councillor of Building since 2016 and has gained a certain reputation as an investors' nightmare. However, the RAW estate is a different story: the Green politician also sees the need for change. Apart from socio-cultural facilities, "there is not much worth preserving there", he explains. But unlike the area to the west of Warschauer Brücke, the eastern side is defined by the district and city councils, rather than the laws of investment. As Schmidt explains, "The RAW estate is exceptional. It has potential."

So is the RAW estate a counterpart to the Ostbahnhof quarter? Instead of being an alien UFO, has the project developed organically, involving the investor, its potential users and the local residents? So far, there have been three dialogue workshops and plenty of visions for the future. The socio-cultural facilities are seeking a compromise with the investor. The Astra Kultur-

haus is looking forward to a new concert hall. Those that have to leave regardless of the outcome are organising protests. And then there are the residents of Revaler Strasse. They not only have to put up with the noise, but also with the 40,000 people a day who flood in from the RAW estate through the Simon-Dach neighbourhood: the down side of tourism. No wonder some people are already talking about the "Berlin Ballermann", a reference to the party zone in Majorca. Nevertheless, a compromise appears to be possible. Schmidt is not even completely opposed to a tower that Kurth intends to build as a counterpart to the tower on the opposite side. If a compromise is reached, it will be the result of the political will to take the strenuous, nerve-racking path of dialogue. It may be the only way to bring together old and new elements in the growing city.

The former wholesale flower market is also located in Friedrichshain-Kreuzberg, albeit at its other end. There is no party tourism there to dictate life in the peaceful southern Friedrichstadt neighbourhood. Largely destroyed during the war, it has experienced wild, heterogeneous development since then, including new buildings, temporary structures, industrial estates and housing construction. The Mehringplatz area in particular has developed into a social hotspot.

Even the southern end of Friedrichstrasse will not remain as it has until now. The neighbourhood will change. All around the Jewish Academy in the large covered market, new construction projects are sending out an urban-planning signal announcing the transformation of the quiet neighbourhood into an artistic, creative quarter. However, the investors involved are by no means Daimler, Zalando or Lauritz Kurth. Instead, joint building ventures aim to show that new development can be done differently.

The ground floor of the Metropolenhaus, with its open project spaces, is subsidised by the sale of apartments above it. The integrative project IBeB uses a similar model to cap the rents for some of the apartments and studios. Another project called Frizz23 regards itself as Berlin's first joint venture group for commercial construction. The *taz* newspaper's new building is also part of the new quarter. Nevertheless, there are still conflicts. Businesses fear higher rents and residents are afraid of being pushed out. But it is not a case of conflict between two fundamentally different worlds. Similarly, new developments are not always confronted by defensive reflexes. "Mehringplatz is like a village", Karin Lücker-Aleman, Managing Director of a neighbourhood café, explains. All the same, she believes the changes in southern Friedrichstadt are necessary. "The greater the mixture, the more ways of life are available. That's an advantage, even for households with low education levels."

Friedrichshain-Kreuzberg continues to be especially attractive due to its wildness, as the Baukollegium confirmed to the district. What once put off investors has become part of its allure. If companies such as Zalando move their headquarters to Kreuzberg, their brands become hip. Investors thereby benefit from Kreuzberg, but does the district benefit from them? At any rate, many people living there fear that such corporate headquarters and the thousands of well-paid employees will force rents up even further. Another aspect is the displacement of temporary and non-commercial uses, although often, they are precisely what paves the way to commercialisation. The results do not look good. Kreuzberg is breaking the ground for those who will in retrospect relegate it to a mere design attribute.

Daniel Wesener, an observer of the building measures on both sides of the Spree, believes there is nevertheless a difference: "Investments are either compatible or incompatible with the city." In the latter case, politics must seek a dialogue, as we can see with the RAW estate, while remaining tough. For instance the State of Berlin intends to build state-owned housing on the grounds where the municipal refuse company is still currently operating. The BSR could move to a plot in Mondersohnstrasse formerly used by the railway. However, Deutsche Bahn currently refuses to sell the property at market value. The district responded as follows: in that case the old warehouses will not

have their preservation-listed status amended and offices will be prohibited in the development plan... Perhaps such statements are more helpful than the desire for "raw and wild" façades. Ultimately however, it is all a question of planning and time. Two decades ago, the legal basis for today's developments was created at a time when many believed it was a good thing that anything at all was happening there. Today, the astonishment is great – as is the will to oppose new implants in the future.

Metropolenhaus by the former wholesale flower market

ZINGSTER reloaded

Zingster Strasse
13051 Berlin

Planning area
740,000 m²

ARGE Zingster reloaded (King, Köhl, Weidinger, Barjenbruch, Naimer)
https://d-nb.info/1078310459/34

New apartment types:
A – Maisonette
B – Apartment with optionally usable room
C – Ground floor apartment
D – Cluster apartment

Rainwater channel

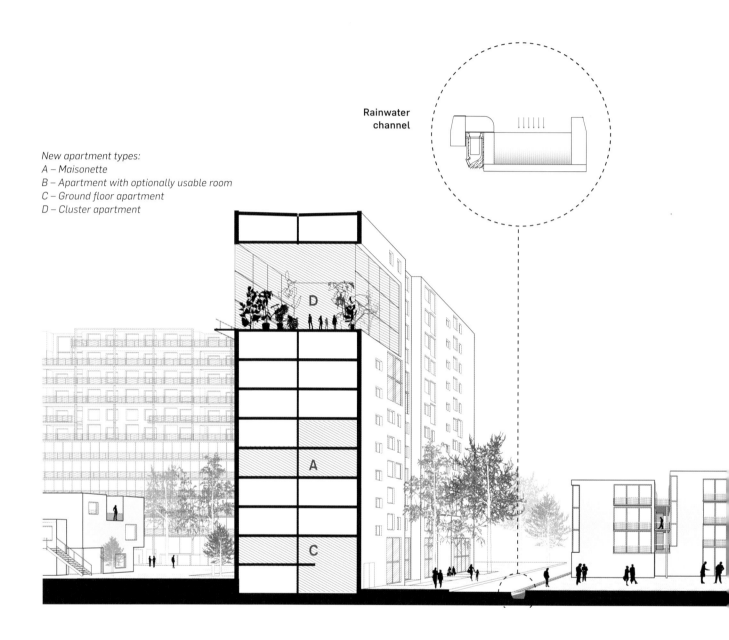

Interdisciplinary research project on the future of a Berlin prefabricated housing estate. The aim is to further develop the area of Zingster Strasse, which was the first building stage of the major monofunctional housing estate in Neu-Hohenschönhausen, into a robust, mixed district. In addition to functional, social and design diversity, there are also questions of sustainability: high-performance open spaces, a sustainable mobility concept and decentralised circulation systems for supply and disposal technology. Thus experts from the disciplines of urban planning, architecture and landscape architecture cooperated with partners from the fields of estate water management and energy technology. Applicable holistic solutions were developed that approach the conversion of the overground and underground city in a synergetic, interdisciplinary way, in a dialogue with the existing urban planning and architectural structures of late Modernity.

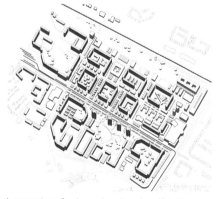

Isometrics of urban planning densification

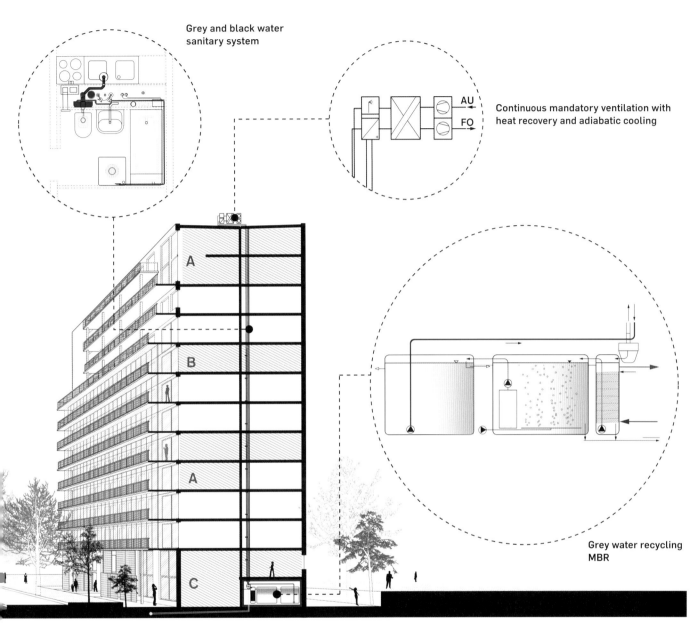

Grey and black water sanitary system

Continuous mandatory ventilation with heat recovery and adiabatic cooling

AU

FO

A

B

A

C

Grey water recycling MBR

Ahrenshooper Strasse: Concept (top) and newly formulated public space (bottom)

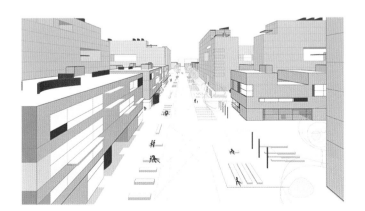

Design handbook for Spandau old town

13597 Berlin

Planning area
570,000 m²

Herwarth + Holz
Planung und Architektur
www.herwarth-holz.de

Contracted by: District of Spandau, Berlin,
Urban Development Authority

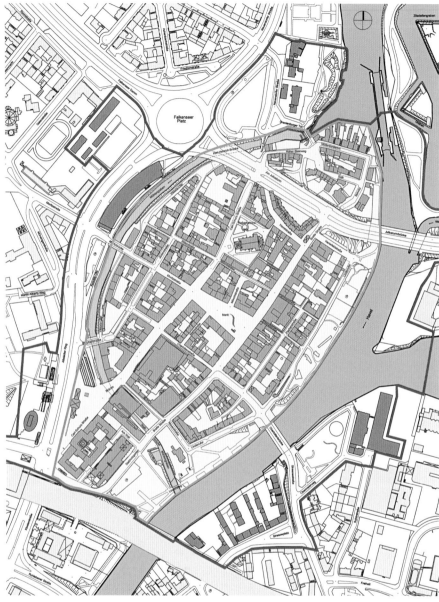

Plan with validity zones

ALTSTADT SPANDAU

GESTALTUNGSHANDBUCH
■ Bebauung   ■ Freiflächen   ■ Werbeanlagen   ■ Sondernutzungen

Overall edition

Design handbook
Preservation regulations

Development of a handbook to preserve and further enhance the location's visual qualities. The overriding aim is to strengthen the important historical old town ensemble as a lively centre for culture, tourism and retailing. The handbook specifies the broader preservation regulations for the compact core of the old town. It provides concrete design rules and recommendations in four fields: building, green and open spaces, advertising and advertisements, and special uses in the street landscape. Urban planning, monumental preservation, economic, process-related and ecological aims are thereby always considered together. This enhances awareness of the characteristic urban planning qualities of the ensemble even more strongly than in the past. At the same time, all participants are made aware of using the existing potential and developing it further through high-quality measures.

Theme: Building

Theme: Green and open spaces

Theme: Advertising and advertisements

Theme: Special uses in the street landscape

Architects, Interior Architects, Landscape Architects and Urban Planners

Authors

Susanne Ehlerding
born 1963, studied Literature and Sociology in Bielefeld, Lille and Berlin, editor of the *Tagesspiegel*, focusing on the energy turn-around and climate change

Heiko Haberle
born 1981, studied Architecture in Berlin and Jerusalem, since 2009 author for exhibitions, magazines and book projects, followed by PR work for an architectural office and the Federal Foundation of Baukultur, since 2016 editor of the *Deutsches Architektenblatt*

Falk Jaeger
born 1950, studied Architecture and History of Art, PhD, Professor of Architectural Theory, freelance architecture critic, curator and publisher in Berlin

Barbara Kerbel
born 1978, studied Psychology in Giessen. She now works as a freelance journalist in Berlin, writing about schools, education, inclusion and language, among others for the *Tagesspiegel*, the Federal Agency for Civic Education and the magazine *Deutsch perfekt*

Maxi Leinkauf
born 1975, studied Politics at the Freie Universität Berlin and SciencesPo Paris; following a traineeship at the *Tagesspiegel*, freelance author, among others for the *Tagesspiegel*, *Cicero*, *Süddeutsche Zeitung* and *Frankfurter Rundschau*, since 2010 editor of *der Freitag*

Friederike Meyer
born 1972, studied Architecture in Aachen and Seattle and Journalism in Berlin. A long-time editor of the magazine *Bauwelt* and since May 2017 editor-in-chief at *BauNetz.de*, she writes and discusses with interested parties about urban and rural issues, architecture and society

Uwe Rada
born 1963, studied German and History, since 1992 editor of the *taz*, responsible for urban development, author of numerous specialist books (including *Hauptstadt der Verdrängung*, *Berliner Barbaren* and *Berlin und Breslau*) and the novel *1988*

Peter Steinhauer
born 1963, studied German, Philosophy and History of Art in Cologne and Bonn, has lived in Berlin since 1996 and works as a freelance journalist in the fields of architecture and design and as an editor of *Cube Berlin* magazine

Photos on page 2 (left to right, top to bottom) **Row 1:** Rainer Gollmer, Andrew Alberts, Till Budde, Udo Meinel, Anna Wietersheim, Marcus Bredt, Werner Huthmacher **Row 2:** Ulrich Schwarz, Lena Wellmann, Laura Hoffmann-Kuhnt, Anastasia Hermann, Christian Gahl, Stefan Müller, Jan Bitter, Allard van der Hoek **Row 3:** Johannes Jakubeit, Paul Ott, Jan Bitter, Tomek Kwiatosz, César Rubio, Wirth Alonso, Frank Bohland **Row 4:** Roman Gericke, ZRS, Christoph Rokitta, platena+jagusch, Werner Huthmacher, Anne Deppe, Branislav Jesić **Row 5:** Rory Gardiner, Michael Moser, Allard van der Hoek, Zeng Jianghe, Linus Lintner, Robert Wählt, Ulrich Schwarz, Oliver Kern **Row 6:** Christo Libuda / Lichtschwärmer, Adrian Birkenmeier / Markus Hemmerich, Aline Calmet, Ali Moshiri, Wolfgang Reiher, Nina Straßgütl, Brigida González **Row 7:** W&V, Stefan Müller, Hans-Christian Schink, Nina Straßgütl, Marcus Ebener, Schnepp Renou, Werner Huthmacher **Row 8:** Philipp von Matt, Marcus Ebener, Martin Meyer, Christo Libuda / Lichtschwärmer, Marc Leppin, Hanns Joosten (3) **Row 9:** Thilo Folkerts, ArchTriumph, Ruven Wiegert, Christian Barthelmes, Bruno Klomfar, capattistaubach, ARGE Zingster reloaded, Carl Herwarth von Bittenfeld

The Deutsche Nationalbibliothek lists this publication in the Deutsche Nationalbibliografie; detailed bibliographic data are available on the Internet at http://dnb.dnb.de.

ISBN 978-3-03768-248-7
ISSN 1439-927X

1st edition 2019
Published by the Berlin Chamber of Architects

Project Selection
Christine Edmaier, architect, Berlin
Brigitte Fehrle, journalist, Berlin
Peter Haimerl, architect, Munich
Dorothée Meier, interior designer, Munich
Oliver Platz, architect, Bremen
Jutta Wakob, landscape architect, Cologne
Jörn Walter, urban planner, Hamburg

Chief Editor
Louis Back

Editorial Coordination
Birgit Koch and Meike Capatti in cooperation with committees of the Berlin Chamber of Architects

Translation
Benjamin Liebelt, Berlin

Layout
eckedesign, Berlin